GREEN AND GOLDEN BOOTS

Australia's overseas golden boot winners

GREEN AND GOLDEN BOOTS

Australia's overseas golden boot winners

JASON GOLDSMITH

FAIRPLAY
PUBLISHING

First published in 2023 by Fair Play Publishing
PO Box 4101, Balgowlah Heights, NSW 2093, Australia
www.fairplaypublishing.com.au

ISBN: 978-1-925914-77-1

ISBN: 978-1-925914-78-8 (ePub)

Cover design and typesetting by Leslie Priestley

Front cover photograph of Sam Kerr celebrating a Chelsea's fifth goal during a UEFA Women's
Champions League group match vs Vllaznia, October 2022, via PA Images/Alamy.
Back cover photograph of Mark Viduka celebrating one of two goals for Celtic against
Dundee United, March 2000, via PA Images/Alamy.

All other photographs are from the personal collections of the individual players,
Kazane Kuwahara of Japan, and Alamy.

All inquiries should be made to the Publisher via hello@fairplaypublishing.com.au

NATIONAL
LIBRARY
OF AUSTRALIA

A catalogue record of this book is available from the National Library of Australia.

Dedicated to my late father Tony,

who instilled in me a love of

sports and gave me all the tools in life

to chase my dreams.

RIP "Fred"

Contents

Foreword
John Kosmina

Everyone loves a goal scorer and Australia has been lucky to produce many fine strikers.

From Timmy Cahill and Sam Kerr in the national teams to Damien Mori and Lisa De Vanna domestically, we have the knack of producing quality footballers who have been able to perform on the big stage.

I was lucky enough to play with the likes of Eddie Krncevic and Frank Farina, be part of coaching teams for Vidmar, Viduka and Kennedy, and then watch from afar admiring the skills and nous of Samantha Kerr.

The one common denominator for most of these big stars we have produced is the Australian Institute of Sport (AIS). Ron Smith set up such a great program that helped kickstart the careers of Farina, Viduka and Kennedy.

Viduka said his entire success was built at the AIS; it is a program we sadly miss today, especially with the growth and success of our Matildas.

In *Green and Golden Boots,* what Jason has put together are some great stories of the individual brilliance of our Aussie footballers in some of the toughest and strangest leagues overseas.

Here's hoping in the future we can add more chapters to these 12 players and have more Australians excel on the world scene.

Kossie

John Kosmina is a former Socceroos' captain. He is in the top 10 all-time goal scorers list for both the Socceroos (42) and the various men's national leagues in Australia over the years. He scored the first ever National Soccer League (NSL) goal in 1977 for West Adelaide at Manuka Oval in Canberra and finished with 133 for his career. He won the 1982 Golden Boot with Sydney City.

Such was his prowess, he was signed by Arsenal in the late 1970s before homesickness brought him back to Australia. He played for West Adelaide, Adelaide City, Sydney City, Sydney Olympic and APIA Leichhardt in the NSL. He also coached the Newcastle Breakers and Brisbane Strikers in the NSL and Adelaide United and Sydney FC in the A-League.

Introduction

According to the International Football Association Board (IFAB) Laws of the Game 2022/23, a goal:

> *'... is scored when the whole of the ball passes over the goal line, between the goalposts and under the crossbar, provided that no offence has been committed by the team scoring the goal.'*

What IFAB cannot define is the *emotion* that goes along with a goal.

Goals are *everything* in football, and the goal scorer usually gets all the glory.

Everyone remembers goals—the scoring team, the defending team, the players and the fans.

Our emotional connection to this moment of euphoria or despair can be linked to those goal-scoring seconds.

From a corner flag-punching Tim Cahill to a backflipping Sam Kerr, these moments are etched in our memories—we remember where we were, how we reacted and who we hugged (if we even knew their names!).

For our national teams, we remember Jimmy Mackay's thunderbolt to send us to the 1974 World Cup, we remember Cahill against Japan in Germany, Leckie against Denmark in Qatar, Kerr's four against Jamaica at the 2019 World Cup and her goal against Great Britain at the Tokyo Olympics. John Aloisi's penalty goal in the 2005 World Cup Qualifier against Uruguay has been seen more times than Mark Schwarzer's equally important—or maybe even more—two penalty saves.

Australia has produced a number of locally based prolific scorers; names we remember who brought in the crowds and wowed fans. Names such as Reg Date, Alf Quill, Lisa De Vanna, Gary Cole, John Kosmina, Damien Mori, Archie Thompson and Jamie Maclaren.

Then there were our pioneers; names like Joe Marston, Ken Grieves, Max Tolson, John Roberts, Craig Johnston, Jim Patikas, John Kosmina and Eddie Krncevic. Australians who bettered themselves by heading overseas and trying their luck in so-called "football countries" where the beautiful game is the number one sport.

From the trickle of Australian footballers who headed overseas in the 1970s and 80s to the flood of homegrown talent who ventured abroad in the 1990s and 2000s, Australia has produced twelve Golden Boot-winning players in overseas leagues. These Aussies have topped the goal tallies in leagues from England to Japan, Belgium to Scotland, and many countries in between.

I believe that we are just getting started.

This book looks at these amazing Australian athletes and their Golden Boot title-winning seasons—from our first pioneer, "the flying kangaroo" Eddie Krncevic's 23 goals for Anderlecht in Belgium in 1988/89 to our most prolific goal scorer in Sam Kerr at Chelsea in 2021/22—she already has five overseas scoring titles and is not done yet!

These stories outline how Aussie footballers look after each other when abroad, and in many cases how these Golden Boot seasons and the publicity around them led to opportunities for many of our footballers to ply their trade in stronger leagues. For example, after winning the Golden Boot, Frank Farina became the first Australian in the Serie A, Mark Viduka went to the Premier League, Adam Taggart to Japan, Clayton Zane to Belgium, Aurelio Vidmar to Holland and Sam Kerr to the UK and potential world domination!

Nothing in the written word can quite capture the emotion of a goal, but in these 12 stories I hope you feel a sense of pride and belonging with Australian footballers and their personal successes.

Chapter 1
Eddie Krncevic
Anderlecht, Belgium, 1988/89 (23 goals)

Eddie Krncevic was born in 1960 in Geelong, Victoria to Croatian immigrant parents. He began his football journey, like many Victorians of Croatian heritage, with the famous Melbourne Knights, then known as Essendon Croatia.

A tall and athletic striker known for his strong skills on the ball and his heading ability, Krncevic was a junior representative in both the Victorian state teams as well as the Under-20 Australian side. He crossed paths in the 1970s with legendary NSL and Socceroo striker Gary Cole, who was coaching the Victorian Under 14 team at the time. Cole recalls a young player who knew he had talent:

'He really impressed me with his confidence as a youngster in the Victorian 14s, and then I got to play against him in the NSL and with him in the Socceroos.'

That confidence led to Krncevic taking all before him domestically in Australia. He started his NSL career with Sydney side Marconi; the teenage talent's debut season saw him winning the NSL title in 1979 in a team that included Golden Boot winner Mark Jankovics (18 goals), Roberto Vieri (Christian Vieri's father) and Socceroos Tony Henderson and Peter Sharne. Krncevic himself would finish second in the Golden Boot with 13 goals and would also win the medal for the best Under-21 player in the competition.

In 1980, he would win the NSL Cup with Marconi and at the end of 1981 he had tallied 81 games for 31 goals.

This period saw Krncevic make his senior debut with the Socceroos and from 1979 to 1981 he would play 33 times for the green and gold. After he left Australia in the early 1980s for an overseas football career he would only feature twice more; in 1989 in two World Cup Qualifiers against Israel.

So, arguably at Krncevic's peak when he was playing club football in Croatia,

Germany, Belgium and France, he didn't get a look in with the Socceroos.

According to Krncevic, he wanted to come back for the big games, such as the World Cup Qualifiers against Scotland in 1985 as well as the Seoul Olympics in 1988, but he wasn't selected.

> 'At the time my club sent a fax saying I was available to play if you play against Scotland, but I was not available for games against the likes of Fiji.
>
> 'They told me they got a reply saying he can't pick and choose his games, so it was quite painful to watch the Scotland game as I feel I could have been influential.'

Scotland defeated Australia 2–0 in Glasgow and a 0–0 draw in Melbourne was enough for them to make the 1986 World Cup, with Australia missing out. The Scotland coach at the time, one Alex Ferguson, even commented that Australia hadn't picked their best player in Krncevic.

Former Socceroos' skipper John Kosmina said they did miss Krncevic but that was football then. Clubs didn't have to release players in FIFA-allocated windows.

> 'We missed Eddie [in 1985] and we also missed David Mitchell and Frank Farina at the end of the 80s.'

Missing the big Socceroo A Internationals later in Krncevic's career was offset by playing against club teams when he was Australia-based earlier on. It put him in the shop window. Krncevic's early Socceroos' games were against big international clubs like New York Cosmos, Fiorentina, Leicester City and Dinamo Zagreb.

Playing against Dinamo Zagreb in Zagreb, Krncevic impressed with his ball play in the snow and a little more than 12 months later, he was convinced to play in Croatia, the birth country of his parents ... and he joined Dinamo Zagreb.

Croatia back in 1981 was part of Yugoslavia and a socialist country. To say it was a culture shock for Krncevic is an understatement. Krncevic was a trailblazer though, he was the first foreigner to play in Yugoslavia.

> 'It was tough, a young guy with Croatian parents coming to a socialist country and they couldn't work out why this kid from Australia was coming over here, so I was followed by the secret police!
>
> 'Not only that, no one would pass the ball to me! I had to work it all out myself!'

Dinamo Zagreb was Krncevic's footballing apprenticeship. He looks back on it now as a great schooling, something that fine-tuned him for his decade in Europe. Zagreb and Croatia are now producing some of the best footballers in the world, but when Krncevic's wife fell pregnant, a new club was needed.

'The moment she said she was pregnant, she said we can't have our child here [Croatia]. She was right as the state of the hospitals was pretty bad.

'That was hard too, because I wasn't sure where I was going to go.'

Krncevic had an offer to go to Greece with Olympiakos and then there was an offer to head to Germany and play with MSV Duisberg. He was seduced by the sales pitch of the Duisberg president.

'The president was a doctor and wasn't going to bother doing a medical and said you will be the first person we sign sight unseen.

'When he rang the Zagreb coach and asked if I was good enough to play in the Bundesliga 2, he said I was good enough to play for Bayern Munich.'

After the birth of his son Jesse, Krncevic wanted to leave Germany because things on the pitch were not working out for him.

'I was a new father which was giving me the drive to be better, but no one was passing me the ball. I got through Yugoslavia and then I wanted to get out of Germany. Sydney Croatia called me and I was interested in going back to the NSL but then the president at Duisberg called me and said there is a Belgian agent that wants to talk to you.'

Krncevic's initial move to Belgium did not go smoothly. The Belgian agent and Cercle Brugge coach Georges Leekens watched him play midweek and then approached him afterwards.

'Leekens said to me in English, "*Do you want to come to Belgium?*", and as I wanted to get out of Germany so badly, I said "*I will run there!*"

Krncevic went to Belgium to trial and his first impressions were not great.

'I scored a goal in the trial but my groin was playing up so I wasn't 100%. Leekens said to me after the game, *"Look, I know what you can do but the others aren't so sure."*

'Then they left me at the hotel without any communication, no food, nothing!

'I was angry and thought, *"I don't want to come to this fucking country again."*

'I came back to Germany and said to my wife, *"I don't want to go there, I was mistreated and felt unwelcome, let's book a holiday."'*

Thinking he would take the family on a nice holiday before a return to Australia to play with Sydney Croatia in the National Soccer League, Krncevic booked a trip to the Canary Islands. But Cercle Brugge had other ideas and tracked him down.

'I got a call from Cercle Brugge while on holiday who said, *"We want to sign you for six months and we will give you X amount of money."* I was so annoyed at how they initially treated me that I was being a bit arrogant and I said, *"No I want this much more,"* and they said, *"Okay, done."'*

He went back to Sydney Croatia briefly for a guest stint, scoring three goals in three games before heading to Belgium to begin what would become a pioneering stint in mainland Europe.

'From the first day, it was a great atmosphere. We had a delay to the start of the season because of the snowfall. So it was two months of pre-season, so I was in great shape, and everyone was passing the ball to me and I felt good.

'I lived in Brugge, which is a beautiful part of the world, and all the boys spoke English.'

Krncevic's Round 1 introduction to Belgian football was when Cercle Brugge came up against powerhouse Anderlecht, and he noticed that his teammates were apprehensive when playing one of the bigger teams. They ended up losing 2–1 and Krncevic was worried that all teams in Belgium would be at that level. He shouldn't have been as he scored in the next game to set the tone for his time in Belgium.

Cercle Brugge won the Belgium Cup that season and with Krncevic scoring important goals along the way (including in that Final), he re-signed for the next season. In that second season they made the Cup Final again and he was making enough of a name in Belgian football that the bigger clubs came knocking at his door.

'Club Brugge and Standard Liège both wanted me, and I signed a pre-contract with Liège to move there. In the interim, I had to go back to Croatia to sort out some business and when I came back to Brussels my agent was there to meet me at the airport and said we are going to Anderlecht.

'I said, *"What about the pre-contract?"* He said, *"Don't worry we will get rid of that."* That's how I got to Anderlecht, the president himself signed me for two years.'

In that first season at Anderlecht, he won the 1986/87 League title. His strike partner was Icelandic star Arnór Guðjohnsen who won the Golden Boot with 19 goals. Krncevic was equal fourth with 16. Guðjohnsen is also famous for being involved in the only father–son combination to play in an international match, when in 1996 he and his son Eiður played in a 3–0 win over Estonia. The then 17-year-old son replaced his 34-year-old father at halftime.

With Krncevic forming a deadly combination up front for Anderlecht, their club success looked set to continue into 1987/88. He was on fire early that season, scoring eight goals in his first six games, including a hattrick, before he got sick. Krncevic was diagnosed with hepatitis A.

'On the Monday at training after my hattrick, I was still sick, so I was referred to a doctor, he thought I had jaundice and said go straight to hospital.

'The hospital came back to me after blood tests and said I had hepatitis A and that I was to rest for a month and said I would probably sleep for two weeks.

'I came home and as soon as I got home that was it, I crashed in bed, think I lost about eight kilograms in three weeks.'

It was a tough road back for Krncevic. It was the final year of his contract and Anderlecht had brought in strikers on loan to cover his loss. A month after his enforced break, he started training again. Within three months he was back playing and even scored in the Final as Anderlecht took out the Belgian Cup to end the season.

Having built a profile in Europe, Krncevic was without a contract for the 1988/89 season and was hoping to stay in Belgium. An incorrect rumour in the local newspaper helped him stay at Anderlecht. Krncevic tells the story:

'Someone wrote in the paper that Paris Saint-Germain was interested in me. I hadn't heard anything about that, but I played it to my advantage.

'The general manager from Anderlecht called me to ask if it was true that PSG were going to sign me and I told him, *"Yes, they have offered a great deal and I am going to sign with them."* Within an hour, the GM had called me back with a better deal to sign for another year at Anderlecht.'

Krncevic was on fire in that 1988/89 season—he scored in his first five games, including a hattrick against Racing Mechelen and a brace against Beerschot. But a twisted ankle threatened to derail his season; Krncevic only netted once in the next ten games.

Once fully fit, he regained his touch and with another season hattrick (this time against Racing Genk) and doubles against Molenbeek, Lierse and Standard Liège, he went into the final game of the season leading the Golden Boot with 22 goals. Second to him was Zvonko Varga of RFC Liège on 16. He had a buffer of six goals which should have been enough, and because it was the final game, the manager wanted to rotate strikers and give Krncevic's teammate Milan Janković a run.

'The manager told me that he thought he might play Milan, as he hadn't played much that season and that I was already our top goal scorer. Milan was a friend of mine and said, *"No, Eddie should finish the season on a high after winning the Golden Boot and play the last game."'*

So Krncevic started and was slow to get into the game, failing to score in the first half. As the Anderlecht boys were coming off at halftime, his left back teammate came up to him to tell him that his rival Varga had scored three first-half goals.

'I asked him how he knew, and he said the crowd are listening to the radio and they are telling him.

'We were playing Cercle Brugge and no one was passing me the ball, but then in the second half the left back, who was telling me what was going on, gave me a long ball on the 18-yard box right on the corner. I was in two minds, I could try to cross it in or I could try to score. I completely mishit it and it went right into the top corner.'

Krncevic's 51st minute goal was his 23rd for the season and lucky for him, it was enough to secure the Golden Boot title. In an amazing final game, Varga scored three second-half goals to go with his first half hattrick. He scored all six in Liège's 6–1 win over Beerschot to finish the season on 22 goals.

Krncevic became the first Australian to win a goal-scoring title overseas. The achievement still fills him with enormous pride.

'My Dad was at that final game, and [it was] a big moment for me, the first Australian to achieve something like that. Probably one of my proudest moments that I was the first one to do it. I was the first one to do a lot of things in football, but that was a big moment for me.'

He would win his second Belgian Cup with Anderlecht that season, and his third overall, scoring goals in all three Cup Final wins.

His goal-scoring antics in Belgium finally got noticed back home and some journalistic pressure on the Socceroos' coach Frank Arok saw Krncevic return to the national team after an absence of eight years. The Socceroos were set to face Israel in two crucial World Cup Qualifiers. They would prove to be Krncevic's Socceroos' swansong.

'I still wasn't getting called back but finally Arok picked me in 1989.

'I was playing in Europe on the Wednesday, then flew to Australia on the Thursday, got in late Friday night, had a small training session on Saturday and then was still quite jetlagged for the Sunday game against Israel.'

The two 1–1 draws against Israel were not enough to clinch the Oceania playoff spot. Israel went on to lose to Colombia who qualified for the 24-team 1990 World Cup in Italy.

After Anderlecht, Krncevic played in France with Mulhouse before returning to Belgium to play with three more clubs in FC Liège, Eendracht Aalst and Charleroi. He finished with 89 League goals in 245 games in Belgium, a figure that swells to well over 100 goals when you count his Cups' success.

Krncevic returned to Australia to finish his playing career in the National Soccer League as a 36-year-old with the Gippsland Falcons under Frank Arok. Post playing, he coached at the highest domestic level in Australia with Carlton, Marconi and South Melbourne.

His playing career in Europe was quite remarkable, but you will find that the assistance he provided to fellow Australians who went to Europe is what really makes him standout as a person.

Many Australian footballers give him credit for helping them move to Europe. Aurelio Vidmar credits Krncevic for helping him settle in Belgium. Frank Farina in his 1998 biography *My World is Round*, written with Bonita Mersiades, and Robbie Slater in his biography *The Hard Way*, written with Matthew Hall, both credit Krncevic too.

'I pretty much helped all the Aussies transition to Belgium. Frank at Club Brugge, I was trying to get him to Anderlecht originally. Paul Okon stayed with me as a 15-year-old for a week. Robbie Slater was at my house nearly every weekend when he was in France and he got to Blackburn through someone that I organised.

'There was also Graham Arnold and Gary van Egmond too. My manager used to take care of me, and then he went and looked after Graham and Gary for no fee.

'I guess I was a bit of a father figure to those boys because I was the first one there. I dealt with a lot of stuff and had a bit of experience there.

'My house was always open to those boys. You got to help people in life.'

A great Australian contributor both on and off the field, "the flying kangaroo" was the catalyst for the next crop of Aussies to make it in Europe. John Kosmina sums up his talent:

'He was unbelievable in the air, a very good header of the ball. Eddie just attacked things in the box and was always there at the end of things.'

Forever welcomed back to Anderlecht, the biggest club in Belgium, Krncevic was inducted into the Football Australia Hall of Fame in the year 2000 and in 2021 was awarded the Medal of the Order of Australia, recognising his outstanding achievements and service for Australia in the sport of football.

Eddie Krncevic | Anderlecht | 1988/89

Round	H or A	Opposition	Score	Result	Goals
1	A	KRC Genk	0-3	W	1
2	A	RWD Molenbeek	0-2	W	1
3	H	Racing Mechelen	6-3	W	3
4	A	VAC Beerschot	1-4	W	2
5	H	RSC Charleroi	2-0	W	1
6	A	KV Kortrijk	2-0	L	0
7	H	RC Liege	1-0	W	0
8	A	KSC Lokeren	2-4	W	0
9	H	Club Brugge	1-0	W	0
10	A	Sint-Truiden	1-1	D	0
11	A	Lierse SK	1-4	W	1
12	H	KV Mechelen	0-0	D	0
13	A	Royal Antwerp	2-1	L	0
14	H	KSV Waragem	2-0	W	Did Not Play
15	A	Standard Liege	2-2	D	Did Not Play
16	H	KSK Beveren	2-0	W	1
17	A	Cercle Brugge	1-3	W	0
18	H	KRC Genk	6-1	W	3
19	H	RWD Molenbeek	4-1	W	2
20	A	Raching Mechelen	0-4	W	1
21	H	VAC Beerschot	3-3	D	0
22	A	RSC Charleroi	0-0	D	0
23	H	KV Kortrijk	2-2	D	1
24	A	RC Liege	2-0	L	0
25	H	KSC Lokeren	5-1	W	1
26	A	Club Brugge	1-1	D	Did Not Play
27	H	Sint-Truiden	2-2	D	0
28	H	Lierse SK	4-2	W	2
29	A	KV Mechelen	1-2	W	0
30	H	Royal Antwerp	1-1	D	0
31	A	KSV Waragem	0-1	W	Did Not Play
32	H	Standard Liege	2-0	W	2
33	A	KSK Beveren	2-4	W	0
34	H	Cercle Brugge	4-2	W	1

Chapter 2
Frank Farina
Club Brugge, Belgium, 1989/90 (23 goals)

Frank Farina's pathway to professional soccer, the Socceroos and international football is quite remarkable given his upbringing.

Of the 948 players who have represented the Socceroos between 1922 to 2022, only one was born in Darwin—Frank Farina.

Of Italian and Torres Strait Islander descent, Farina spent his early childhood years in Papua New Guinea before moving to Cairns in Far North Queensland.

Far North Queensland doesn't fare much better than Darwin when it comes to Socceroos' representatives, with only six players born in the region having made it through. But as a plucky teenager with Queensland State League side Mareeba United, a 16-year-old Farina caught the attention of Australian Institute of Sport (AIS) coach Jimmy Shoulder in the most peculiar fashion.

Having missed out on selection for the Queensland Under-17 team, Farina was asked to head to a training camp for coaches in Brisbane. The coaches needed players to help with drills and match simulations. Shoulder was there in his role for the AIS and he saw something in Farina. He offered him a scholarship on the spot to attend the AIS.

Having never made any representative sides in his junior career, it was some kind of achievement for the 16-year-old Farina to attend the AIS in 1982.

Farina combined his football education at the AIS with high school in Canberra and started to represent Australia at underage level. In 1983, as an 18-year-old, he went to the Under-20 World Cup in Mexico, famously scoring against the hosts in front of over 100,000 people.

He joined Canberra City for two seasons in the National Soccer League before the rich Sydney clubs came knocking. Farina would join Sydney City for the 1985 and 1986 seasons before he really came into his own at Marconi in 1987 and 1988. Former

Socceroos' striker Gary Cole describes the type of player Farina was:

'Technically very good, he got a lot of benefit from his pace, he could come back and play wide. He played up front out wide in the early days and then learned to play inside. He was strong, quick and aggressive but would have been outgunned by tall tough defenders so had to rely on silky skills. A very good finisher.'

Always a prolific goal scorer, Farina would win the NSL Golden Boot in 1987 with 16 goals, and he made it back-to-back scoring titles with another 16 in 1988. Marconi also won the NSL title that year, and Farina was named Oceania Player of the Year and had a major impact at the 1988 Seoul Olympics.

The Olympic Football competition was not yet an Under-23 competition in 1988 and the teams that competed were senior national teams. Under Frank Arok, the Socceroos defeated Yugoslavia 1–0 at the Olympics with Farina netting the winner. The increasing exposure of the Socceroos with the Olympic Qualifiers, Olympic Games results like the win against Yugoslavia, and tournaments such as the Bicentennial Gold Cup put Farina into the international shop window.

With clubs knocking on his door, Farina decided to head to Belgium. He joined Club Brugge alongside fellow Aussie Vlado Bozinovski.

Belgium football was in a strong position in the late 1980s with their national team having made the 1986 World Cup Quarter-Finals. Farina would join a club team that had six Belgian internationals, including Jan Ceulemans who was the skipper of both Club Brugge and the national team.

The transition to Europe was made easier by him heading over with his partner at the time and gaining some support from Eddie Krncevic, as Farina recalls.

'When I went to Europe, the only Aussies that were there were Eddie, and Dave Mitchell was in Scotland.

'Eddie and I caught up whenever we could, he played for Cercle Brugge so he knew the town, he was a big help to me when I moved there.'

Coming into Club Brugge midway through the 1988/89 season, Farina managed around 15 games under manager Henk Houwaart. With six foreigners on their books, it was hard to make the top three foreigners allowed to play in the first team.

Season 1989/90 was a watershed one for both Farina and Club Brugge. They had replaced Houwaart with Georges Leekens. Leekens was manager of Cercle Brugge when Krncevic went to Belgium so Farina knew what he was like, thanks to conversations with his fellow Aussie.

Bozinovski wasn't wanted by Leekens and after six games at Club Brugge, he left to play in Portugal. Leekens was a champion player at Club Brugge in the 1970s, even featuring in Champions League Finals.

However, his initial relationship with Farina was frosty. During the pre-season, Leekens and Farina clashed regarding team selection, with Farina spending a lot of time on the bench.

'He wasn't going to play me, he said I was free to leave. As it panned out, I ended up starting in the first game of the season.'

Fighting for foreign spots in the first team at the time was ruthless, but Leekens gave Farina the nod for Round 1 against Standard Liège.

Farina got off the mark in Round 3 when he scored against Mechelen and over the next ten games he would score eight more times—including doubles against Gent and Waragem. He never looked back.

With three rounds to go in the season, Farina scored in the Brugge derby as Club Brugge beat Cercle 2–0.

The most games Farina went without scoring that season was only four; not bad in a 34-game season where he played in 33 and scored 23 goals. The next best was 18 goals to Marc Degryse from Anderlecht. Farina won the Golden Boot title in his first full season in Belgium.

Not only did he win the goal-scoring title, but he managed to score at home in the second last round of the season as Club Brugge defeated Sint-Truidense 3–0 to win the title with a game to spare.

Famously, the supporters stormed the pitch and an unsuspecting Farina was stripped of his kit. He returned to the changerooms with only one sock and his speedos! He recalls the situation:

'I scored in the game against St Trudiense to win at home and clinch the League.
'Jan Cuelemans was my captain and he was saying to me with ten minutes to go *"Frankie, get off the field quickly at the end,"* and I just didn't understand what he was on about.

'When the final whistle blew, he started running to the rooms with some of the other players, I was just standing there with my arms up in the air celebrating to the crowd.

'Then people just started jumping the fences and started running on the field. It was all in good spirits, supporters were hugging me and kissing me and saying give me this, give me that.

'First thing was my shirt, then someone said, *"Please give us your shorts!"* and I was like, *"Seriously? Come on!"* They were grabbing me and patting me on the back and I had more scratches on me than from the game. I took my pants off and then my boots and then one sock.

'When I got into the rooms, I only had on one sock and my swimming togs—I used to wear those budgie smugglers when I played.

'They got my shirt, my shorts, my boots and one sock. It was quite funny to be honest—and all in good fun. It was just a sea of people celebrating on the pitch.'

With Belgium having one eye on the 1990 World Cup in Italy and Club Brugges having so many national team players, the 1989/90 season was a perfect storm for Farina to play good football and be involved in a successful side.

One of the Club Brugges sponsors was Moët & Chandon and to celebrate the 1989/90 title, the whole team got treated to a day out at their French headquarters.

'After we won the title we still had one game to play, but after the season finished we had a day trip to the Moët factory in France, just over the Belgian border.

'We got a big bus that took us there, we were all in suits, we got a tour around the factory and all around the cellars, then they gave us a magnum each as we were leaving!

'Everyone kept their magnum, but they did give us extras which the boys took to on the bus, so you can imagine the state of us when we got back to Brugge. Everyone drinking champagne!'

Club Brugges finished the following season in 1990/91 in fourth place; however the season was still deemed a success as they won the Belgian Cup. Farina scored 12 goals that year.

Belgium proved to be a stepping stone for bigger things for Farina. His next club was Bari in the Italian Serie A. Although Bari was not a massive club, it was another barrier that Farina would smash in his career. He became the first Australian to play in Italy's top-flight competition.

A change of coach at Bari shortened Farina's time in Italy. Rules on foreign players only allowed for three and with England captain David Platt and Croatian international Zvonimir Boban on the books, when new coach Zbigniew Boniek wanted to bring in another Croatian (defender Robert Jarni), Farina's opportunities were limited. A potential transfer to Sheffield Wednesday didn't happen and after featuring nine times for Bari, Farina was loaned out to English side, Notts County.

As more Aussies made it to Europe, Farina was able to catch up with a few more mates, spending time with Fred De Jong and Graham Arnold in Holland as well as Robbie Slater in France. The camaraderie was great as they could all understand the struggles of being an Australian trying to find their way in European football.

After Bari, Farina moved to France where he would enjoy three seasons in Ligue 1, playing for Strasbourg and Lille before a return to Australia's National Soccer League and the Brisbane Strikers.

John Kosmina saw first-hand how good a footballer Farina was and rated his football even higher when he returned from overseas.

'Frank was lightning quick, he would get in behind all the time, [he was] very aggressive in a good way.

'Going overseas made Frank. He scored a lot of goals in Australia before he left. I played with him at Sydney City, against him when he was at Marconi, and with him in the national team. He was always good for a goal—he was a natural goal scorer but his finishing and his touch improved out of sight after he went overseas.'

The Brisbane Strikers started Farina's managerial career. His second season with them in 1996/97 was as their player/manager and he won the title, scoring a goal in their 2-0 win over Sydney United at a sold-out Lang Park.

Farina would go on to coach Marconi and then take the Socceroos' job, leading the national team 58 times, more than any other Socceroos' coach to date.

He had club stints coaching in the A-League with Brisbane Roar and Sydney FC before jobs managing Papua New Guinea and Fiji.

Recognised by Australia's Professional Football Association with their Alex Tobin Medal, Farina was the fifth recipient after Joe Marston, Johnny Warren, Craig Johnston and Mark Viduka. The medal is awarded for outstanding attributes—leadership, achievement as a player, commitment to one's fellow professionals, and service and dedication to the game.

In November 2021, he was appointed to the inaugural National Indigenous Advisory Group of Football Australia. This group supports Indigenous players and aims to increase their participation.

Farina returned to Brugge in 2022. With fellow Aussie Paul Okon working as an assistant coach there, it was easy for him to reconnect with teammates and people from his past.

'I rang Paul. He has a restaurant there as well as being an assistant coach, and he said *"Brilliant, I am going to organise a dinner for you."*

'The godfather of my son is still in Brugge as my son was born there, so I got to Brugge and Paul opened his restaurant up and invited five players from my era. All these players came with their wives and we had a great dinner. It was fantastic.'

Not only did he catch up with former teammates in Brugge but he had a chance encounter with another special friend as well.

'On the last night that we were there, we booked into one of my favourite restaurants in the centre of Brugge, a popular and high-profile restaurant that is still around over thirty years later.

'The guy who owned the restaurant back in the day still owned it, so I booked a table and when we got in there, I got a tap on the shoulder from the owner who goes *"Frankie, you're not going to believe who just walked in, Georges Leekens!"*

'I said, *"You're kidding!"*, I turned around. He sat down, so I went over and tapped him on the shoulder, and he turned around and goes, *"Bloody!"*, that was his nickname for me. After that, it was on. We had a great chat and a wonderful evening with him.

'That is Brugges. I always say, *"It's my city mate!"*'

Frank Farina | Club Brugge | 1989/90

Round	H or A	Opposition	Score	Result	Goals
1	A	Standard Liege	1-1	D	0
2	H	KV Kortrijk	1-1	D	0
3	A	KV Mechelen	3-1	L	1
4	H	KAA Gent	4-1	W	2
5	A	Germinal Ekeren	2-2	D	0
6	H	RSC Charleroi	1-0	L	1
7	H	Lierse SK	2-0	W	1
8	A	KSK Beveren	0-1	W	0
9	H	RC Liege	2-0	W	1
10	A	KSV Waragem	1-3	W	2
11	H	Royal Antwerp	0-2	L	0
12	A	Racing Mechelen	1-2	W	1
13	H	KSC Lokeren	3-1	W	0
14	A	RSC Anderlecht	0-0	D	0
15	H	Cercle Brugge	2-1	W	Did Not Play
16	A	Sint-Truiden	1-4	W	2
17	H	VAC Beerschot	3-0	W	1
18	H	Standard Liege	2-1	W	1
19	A	KV Kortrijk	0-3	W	0
20	H	KV Mechelen	3-0	W	1
21	A	KAA Gent	2-2	D	1
22	H	Germinal Ekeren	4-0	W	0
23	A	RSC Charleroi	0-1	W	1
24	A	Lierse SK	1-5	D	1
25	H	KSK Beveren	2-0	W	0
26	A	RC Liege	0-0	D	0
27	H	KSV Waragem	3-0	W	0
28	A	Royal Antwerp	0-4	W	0
29	H	Racing Mechelen	4-0	W	1
30	A	KSC Lokeren	0-3	W	2
31	H	RSC Anderlecht	3-0	W	1
32	A	Cercle Brugge	0-2	W	1
33	H	Sint-Truiden	3-0	W	1
34	A	VAC Beerschot	0-0	W	0

Chapter 3
Aurelio Vidmar
Standard Liège, Belgium, 1994/95 (22 goals)

Aurelio Vidmar is a South Australian and a Socceroos' legend. He had one of the most famous manes in Australian football and famously scored against Maradona's Argentina in a World Cup Qualifier at a packed-out Sydney Football Stadium in October 1993.

Vidmar also had a 20-year professional career, book-ended with stints in his hometown of Adelaide. He plied his trade overseas with clubs in Belgium, the Netherlands, Switzerland, Spain and Japan. He was the third Australian to play in Belgium and the third Australian overall to win a Golden Boot when he scored 22 goals for his third Belgian club, Standard Liège, in the 1994/95 season.

Vidmar and his younger brother Tony earned their stripes by developing their football locally in Australia's National Soccer League with Adelaide City. The South Australian club was initially formed through Italian migrants and used to be called Adelaide Juventus.

With over 150 games at Adelaide City, including the 1986 title as a 19-year-old, Vidmar decided to try his luck in Belgium in the early 1990s.

Although the trail had been blazed a few seasons prior by both Krncevic and Farina, it still wasn't a smooth path for Australian footballers hoping to make their mark in Europe. Vidmar had to trial, and he started his journey with club Germinal Ekeren.

'I went for a week-long trial there in '91 and was told by the coach that they wouldn't take me but then I had the opportunity to go to another Belgian club in Kortrijk who signed me.

'Ironically after that first year that I missed out at Ekeren, they signed my brother Tony after the '92 Olympics. It was the same coach that knocked me back! Tony left after three months as he wasn't happy there.'

Like many Aussies that ventured to Europe, Vidmar lent on Krncevic.

> 'I spoke to Eddie a few times when I first went there so he explained to me how it all worked, which was invaluable. Eddie and Frank Farina were legends, both of them, and Paul Okon [Belgian Footballer of the year with Club Brugge in 1995/96] were [all] very well liked.'

Vidmar scored ten goals in his debut Belgian season, but despite that, Kortrijk finished 17th and was one of the bottom three sides who were relegated.

Wanting to remain in the Belgian First Division, Vidmar got a lifeline from neighbouring Waregem, a club just 15 kilometres down the road. It was a smooth transition. Vidmar had a great season—he ended up scoring 19 goals, three ahead of fellow Aussie Graham Arnold who was playing for RC Liège. Waregem also qualified for European football that season after finishing the season in fourth spot.

In season 1993/94, Vidmar was coming into the prime age for a striker and he was in his third season in Belgium. He thought he was starting to make it as a European footballer, but his passion to play for the Socceroos would hold him back at club level. Without FIFA-allocated windows where clubs had to release players for international fixtures, Vidmar would play for Australia, then return to club land and seemingly have to start from scratch again. This scenario would play out across Europe for many of Australia's footballers.

> 'I always wanted to go back and play for my country—they all knew that but they were still a little pissed off. A lot of the times when I came back, I had to come back through the reserves, that was part and parcel of playing for the Socceroos and the clubs' so-called punishment. But within a few weeks you would be back in the first team. I didn't care, I wanted to play with the national team.'

Playing for Australia during this time is when Vidmar was involved in the high-profile, two-legged playoff against Argentina for the final spot at the 1994 World Cup to be held in the USA. It felt like the whole football world was watching these playoffs as they marked the return to the Argentinian national team of the most famous footballer in the world at that time—Diego Maradona. In the first tie, Maradona crossed the ball for Balbo to open the scoring for Argentina before Vidmar scored the equaliser six minutes later. What made the goal even more special for Aurelio was the ball being crossed in by his brother, Tony.

After a 1–1 draw with Argentina in the first leg, the Australians lost the second leg 1–0 to miss qualifying for the 1994 World Cup.

Aurelio Vidmar's travelling to play for the Socceroos (and Waregem playing him in the reserves on his return) took their toll and the club struggled that season. Three weeks before the end of the season, and for the second time in three years for Vidmar, his club was relegated.

'There were some problems inside the club and the atmosphere wasn't great, and I didn't want to be in the Second Division. So, I had to find a new club.'

As luck would have it, the new coach of Standard Liège was Robert Wasiege, a man who had watched Vidmar the past three seasons when he was coach of Charleroi and RC Liège. He wanted Vidmar and Aurelio was happy to sign.

'They were one of the top three clubs at the time with Anderlecht and Club Brugge. We had a tough-arse fitness coach for our pre-season who was a decathlete. I lost count of the number of hurdles and 100-metre runs and 50-metre sprints we had to do.

'I felt very, very strong, I didn't miss a day of pre-season and right from the first game I scored a hattrick against Antwerp and it took off from there.'

In what was a great way to announce his arrival at a new club, Standard Liège played Royal Antwerp in a standalone Friday night fixture to start the season. Vidmar scored in the fifth minute and again in the 68th and 87th minutes to ensure a 3–1 win.

With six goals in the first four rounds, Vidmar was in fine form leading into the Liège derby. Standard Liège's arch-rival was RC Liège and they had fellow Australian Graham Arnold playing for them.

'That was a massive deal. They were a little bit like Man City and Man U, you wanted to be the team of the city that would get the win, otherwise it was a bit difficult to go outside in Liège, where they are just fanatical.'

Scoring a penalty in a 1–1 draw away, Vidmar would go on to win the hearts of the Standard Liège faithful by scoring the winner in a 1–0 home win in the return match.

Despite the rivalry, Vidmar would often catch up with Graham Arnold as they were living in the same town. Other Aussies in Belgium at the time were Paul Okon (Club Brugge) and the Aloisi brothers Ross (FC Boom) and John (Royal Antwerp).

'Arnie invited me to his house many times, and to combat homesickness we would have sausage rolls for dinner!

'John Aloisi was at Antwerp. We hung around a helluva lot as well, especially on our days off.'

The number of Adelaide City boys bouncing around Belgium at the time was quite amazing.

Despite a great start to the season with 17 goals in the first 23 games, Vidmar then had a dry spell of eight consecutive games without scoring. But the lack of a VAR (Video Assistant Referee) and some rat cunning saw him break the dry spell with his own version of a Maradona moment.

'I remember the dry spell, I couldn't hit a barn door from five yards out. Typically with goal scorers you're in a purple patch or a rough patch and I was in a rough patch.

'I remember the first goal that I got back into form was that one against KV Brethren where there was a long ball and the goalkeeper ran out. He and I were going 50/50 and because it was head high, I actually used my hand to punch it away from the keeper, a little tap near my face. I tapped the ball around the keeper and went around him and one of their defenders was on the goal line, so I had the whole goal to myself and luckily I smashed it and it went through his legs.

'They all complained that it was handball but I got away with it, and then the goal-scoring form turned around quickly after that.'

Vidmar's hair at the time was fashionably-long and his flowing mane may have disguised the punch from the referee. But it seemed to break his dry spell. He finished the season with five goals in the last three games, including a brace in the final round against Club Brugge to win the Golden Boot by one goal.

'I have to thank my teammate Marc Wilmots for that second goal against Brugge, because he was such an unselfish and generous player.

'He was in front of the goal, all by himself, and he actually passed it to me instead of scoring himself. That was the type of player he was, he was aware of what was going on.

'The funny thing was that Paul Okon was there on the line trying to stop the ball and I actually put it through his legs.'

Playing against Club Brugge in that final game, Standard Liège were still a chance for the title, vying with powerhouse Anderlecht but needing them to lose or draw against Gent. 0–0 scores at halftime of both games meant Vidmar was still fighting for the championship into the last 45 minutes of the season. But it was not to be. According to Vidmar, they had probably cost themselves the title a week before.

'We were two points clear with a few rounds to go when we went to Anderlecht and lost 2–1. That was a turning point for us, we didn't recover from that.'

Vidmar finished the season on 22 goals, one ahead of Gilles De Bilde of Aalst. RFC Seraing's Roger Lukaku, father of Romelu, was equal third with 15.

The 1994/95 Golden Boot was a magnificent individual honour for Vidmar. He was also awarded the Oceania Footballer of the Year in 1994. Long-time admirer and mentor John Kosmina said:

'Viddy was a skilful player, he would have been different to Frank and Eddie in Belgium in that he was more of a touch player. He wasn't an out and out striker like the others.

'He played like a number 10, he always came off between the lines. He wasn't the sort of player to back into the centre-backs and hold the ball up, that wasn't his game. He was always facing forward and he made great runs into the box, the timing of his runs was exceptional. He was a great finisher.'

Not only was being a foreigner in Europe a tough ask, but the rules of the time also made things harder. Vidmar explains.

'Back in those days, it was very difficult for the strikers because you could still tackle from behind. Most games you would come off with stud marks down your calves or your Achilles.'

Vidmar's breakout season proved to be a stepping stone as he signed with Dutch powerhouse Feyenoord for the following season. While his remaining career in Europe was not as successful as his season with Standard Liège, he nonetheless played with Sion in Switzerland and Tenerife in Spain before heading to Sanfrecce Hiroshima in Japan.

Vidmar returned to Australia and amassed over 100 games with Adelaide City in the NSL before finishing his career with Adelaide United in the A-League.

His contribution to Australian football continued into the coaching ranks, working as an assistant with Adelaide United and the Socceroos as well as having senior coaching gigs with the Australian Under-20 and Under-23 teams. He also had a caretaker coaching role for the Socceroos ahead of Ange Postecoglou's appointment.

He has only been back to Belgium and Liège once.

'The only time I have been back to Belgium and Liège was when I was with the Socceroos and they were playing Belgium. My ex-teammate Marc Wilmot was the Belgian coach. It was nice to see some familiar faces and great to see Marc as well!'

As of 2023, Vidmar was still coaching professionally in Thailand with Bangkok United.

Aurelio Vidmar | Standard Liege | 1994/95

Round	H or A	Opposition	Score	Result	Goals
1	H	Royal Antwerp	3-1	W	3
2	A	KV Mechelen	0-2	W	0
3	H	Sint-Truiden	2-0	W	1
4	A	RSC Charleroi	0-3	W	2
5	A	RC Liege	1-1	D	1
6	H	RWD Molenbeek	1-1	D	0
7	A	KV Oostende	0-2	W	1
8	H	KAA Gent	2-0	W	Did Not Play
9	A	Cercle Brugge	3-0	L	0
10	H	Germinal Ekeren	2-0	W	0
11	A	Lommel SK	3-0	L	0
12	H	Lierse SK	2-0	W	1
13	A	Eendracht Aalst	1-3	W	2
14	H	RSC Anderlecht	1-1	D	0
15	A	KSK Beveren	2-2	D	1
16	H	RFC Seraing	1-0	W	0
17	A	Club Brugge	2-0	L	Did Not Play
18	A	Royal Antwerp	0-1	W	0
19	H	KV Mechelen	3-1	W	1
20	A	Sint-Truiden	1-1	D	0
21	H	RSC Charleroi	2-0	W	2
22	H	RC Liege	1-0	W	1
23	A	RWD Molenbeek	1-2	W	1
24	H	KV Oostende	2-0	W	0
25	A	KAA Gent	0-1	W	0
26	H	Cercle Brugge	2-0	W	0
27	A	Germinal Ekeren	1-1	D	0
28	H	Lommel SK	1-0	W	0
29	A	Lierse Sk	0-0	D	0
30	H	Eendracht Aalst	0-0	D	0
31	A	RSC Anderlecht	2-1	L	0
32	H	KSK Beveren	4-1	W	2
33	A	RFC Seraing	1-1	D	1
34	H	Club Brugge	2-0	W	2

Chapter 4
Scott Ollerenshaw
Sabah FA, Malaysia, 1995 (22 goals)
Sabah FA, Malaysia, 1996 (18 goals)

Scott Ollerenshaw's talent was identified early in his career. He played in all of the St George youth teams growing up, for the National Schoolboys team in 1985, and he debuted in the National Soccer League with St George as an 18-year-old in 1986 before representing the Young Socceroos in 1987.

Frank Arok was Ollerenshaw's coach at club level with St George, a position he held at the same time as being coach of the Socceroos. Arok was an admirer of Ollerenshaw's pace, and it led to his early call up for the national team. Ollerenshaw first played for the senior Socceroos in 1987. He then featured in some big games in Socceroos' history. He played against both Brazil and Argentina in the 1988 Bicentennial Gold Cup, featured at the 1988 Seoul Olympics against Nigeria and his final two appearances for the Socceroos were in two World Cup Qualifying games against New Zealand in 1989, aged just 21. However, once Arok moved on as coach, he didn't get called up again.

After St George, Ollerenshaw moved across town to fellow NSL side Sydney Olympic for a couple of seasons and then to APIA Leichhardt. In 1992/93, the opportunity came for him to move to the UK to join Walsall, who were then playing in the fourth tier, now known as League Two.

Despite the football culture of the United Kingdom, Ollerenshaw didn't want to stay there, describing his 20-game stint in the West Midlands as the "coldest year of my life." He returned to Australia to play with the Wollongong Wolves.

Around that time, Australian players Abbas Saad and Alistair Edwards were playing in Singapore in the Malaysian League and Ollerenshaw was trying to find a way to join them. Soon afterwards, Alan Davidson, John Hunter, Mehmet Duraković and Marshall Soper were all playing there as well.

In the 1990s it wasn't easy to transfer to Malaysia. You needed to trial and with each club being allowed only three foreigners, spots were limited. Most clubs used the foreigners to form the spine of the team, a centre-back, a creative midfielder and a forward, so it took Ollerenshaw a few trials before he found a club that wanted him.

'Alan Davidson organised a trial for me, so I went over there, played in the trial, scored two goals from memory but they didn't sign me. I remember thinking they are hard markers.

'Then player agent Lesley Armstrong called me and said come to Kuala Lumpur and have a trial there. They were coached by a guy called Ken Shellito, ex-Chelsea player and manager. I went down there, played the trial game and scored two goals again.

'Ken came up to me after the game and said you played really well but I don't need a striker, I need a centre-back so I said, "*Well, what am I doing here?*", and he said, "*I'm not sure.*" He ended up signing an Aussie centre-back named Scott O'Donnell.'

Unsuccessful, Ollerenshaw returned to Australia and went back to the Wolves to play in the National Soccer League. After trialling in Malaysia on the Tuesday and Thursday, he returned to Australia on the Friday before playing Heidelberg away in Melbourne on the Sunday. By his own admission, he didn't play very well—he was exhausted.

The next day, Lesley Armstrong called him again, this time saying Malaysian club Sabah needed a striker and could he fly back for another trial. Ollerenshaw was quite reluctant to trial again, feeling that two goals per trial game was enough to show what he could do, but Armstrong was persistent, telling him that his trial form was why Sabah were keen. So Ollerenshaw flew to Malaysia for yet another trial. He didn't set the world on fire, but he did earn a contract!

'I flew to Sabah on the Monday, played in the trial game on the Wednesday, played like a busted arse and didn't score. I played shit but they signed me straight away.'

Released from Wollongong with a transfer fee, Ollerenshaw signed for Sabah for the 1994 season and he has lived there ever since.

He had a breakout debut season with Sabah in 1994, scoring over 20 goals as the club finished fourth and were runners-up in the 1994 Malaysian FA Cup.

In 1995, Sabah won the Malaysian FA Cup 3–1 against Pahang in front of 40,000 fans—Ollerenshaw scoring in what was a breakout evening for him in the League.

Not long afterwards, the Liga Perdana/Malaysian Super League would be rocked by match-fixing allegations and scandal that would see over 150 players arrested. Only players were arrested, but it was alleged that team owners, coaches and even physiotherapists were all in on the corruption.

Canadian Dr Declan Hill is a leading expert on match fixing and corruption in international sport. He wrote the book *The Fix* on football match fixing and he described the situation facing Ollerenshaw when the football competition was in complete disarray.

'Match fixing was part of their footballing culture for decades from at least 1986.

'There was a diplomatic government wrangle, between Singapore and Malaysia, because they were sharing the League and the Singaporeans said that it's the Malaysians that are fixing and the Malay guys were saying it's the Singaporeans.

'They were literally having a fight; [the] problem was they were both right. The entire League was corrupt.

'The Malaysian home minister at the time estimated that 70% of the games had been fixed.'

Hill recalled speaking with Ollerenshaw about the trauma of being involved with these games and the toll it was taking.

'I remember Scott telling me that in one game he scored three or four goals and then a couple of weeks later they discover[ed] that the game was fixed. He told me he pulled the car over to the side of the road and he cried and had this emotional moment thinking how much of that was real?'

After Sabah had won the FA Cup, manager Kelly Tham was sacked along with six of their players after the match-fixing allegations. Most of the players tasked with filling the void in the team came from the club's Under-23 side. Sabah needed a coach, someone who could work with young players, so Ollerenshaw recommended to their manager that they approach the head of the Australian Institute of Sport (AIS) football program, Ron Smith. "Olly" made the call, pleading for some help. Smith remembers it well.

'I never had a close relationship with Olly but he rang me and said, *"Would you be available to come out to Malaysia for three months and try and help us out of a hole?"* He explained to me that they had lost players to match fixing, they had barely won a game and were second to bottom.

'He said he had talked to their president about trying to get someone like me to coach the team because they had a whole lot of players from their Under-23's squad in their first team.

'He asked, *"Can you please come to teach these players and try to organise them? We have eight games left."*

As luck would have it, Smith was about to take ten weeks' long service leave that was forced upon him due to working through summer NSL seasons and winter AIS football programs. Sabah were also travelling to Brisbane to play some trial games at the same time as the Malaysian national team was in camp. Smith was going to be in Brisbane to scout some youngsters for the AIS. He agreed to chat to Sabah's management.

'I met with their president to have a chat. He said if you could come out for three months, that would be brilliant. I changed my long service leave to 12 weeks and took the job.'

Smith's coaching debut with Sabah was a baptism of fire as they took on League heavyweights Pahang, who had Australian legend Alan Davidson and half the Malaysian national team in their ranks. They were the competition benchmark and they whipped Sabah 4-0.

With Smith thinking *'What have I done?',* he spent a sleepless night after the game in front of the whiteboard working out what he could do to change the club's fortunes. A change of tactics to focus on defence first and stopping goals was derived. Smith explained:

'I moved our Serbian midfielder to the central striker role and played Olly and another speedster on the wings, and in the remaining seven games we drew one and won six and came fifth in the League. That qualified us for the Malaysia Cup!'

Ollerenshaw finished the season as the Golden Boot winner with 22 goals for the season, but he wasn't too impressed with being moved to the wing again. Smith remembered:

'Olly came to me and said he wasn't happy, all his life he wanted to play in the middle and score goals, but because he was quick and could cross well he'd always been played on the wing.

'He said he left Australia to try and carve a career for himself up front, and I've asked him to do what he vowed he didn't want to do again.

'Being a redhead he was always a bit fiery, he was grumpy about that. I told him it wasn't a life sentence—it was for a short space of time to get out of this mess.'

With most teams forced to play new players due to all the match-fixing bans, the competition became a little more intense. According to Declan Hill:

'The lion's share of fixers were the Malay and Singapore lads. The games were played harder after the bans, the players were taking things seriously because they didn't want to end up in a jail somewhere.'

Smith was asked to return in 1996 with Sabah and he had no hesitation in signing on again.

'I was hooked on the atmosphere. When I got there, the crowd was 3,000 but in the Cup there was a full house of 23,000. I just loved it, it was what football was about—winning games and being competitive, it gets everyone involved.

'The salary at Sabah was quadruple that of the AIS, plus bonuses, accommodation and a car. The challenge was there, but financially it was too hard to say no.'

Smith's achievements with the Sabah team were impressive—after saving them from a dire situation, he took them to the title in 1996. Ollerenshaw said they still talk about Sabah's golden era.

'Ronny came in and had to start from scratch, he brought in about seven kids and that started Sabah's run… They still talk about it which is a bit of a blight on the situation now. 1995 we won the FA Cup, 1996 we won the League and Malaysia Cup Final, 1997 we came 2nd in the League.'

Smith didn't recruit any new players on his return, relying on Ollerenshaw and the locals.

'I came back in '96 and we won the League and we didn't sign any other players to do so. When people ask me what is one of your greatest achievements in football, I say well *that* was. It was the same group that was there when I took over.

'We brought in some local lads from the villages but no one really into the squad. I moved Olly up front and the more I saw of him, the more I saw he was right. He needed the freedom to move. We worked on the timing of his runs and when to make his runs to maximise his pace.

'He was great to work with, keen as mustard and would always want to talk about how to make him a better footballer.'

Ollerenshaw still needed the coaching and guidance from Smith. In 1996, despite Sabah starting the season well, he couldn't find the back of the net.

'I remember I was in a drought and then I scored one in the tenth game and then went on a run where I kept scoring.'

In that 1996 title-winning season, Ollerenshaw would finish the season on 18 goals and win his second successive Golden Boot.

Ollerenshaw scored more than a goal a game in over 100 appearances for Sabah and Smith recognised a player who always wanted to do more.

'The more I got to know him, he was amazing. He would do his own training, his own match preparation. He and the other two foreigners were great role models for the local boys. They were what they preached, they were well disciplined, and they made no secret that they were doing their own thing for every match. It rubbed off on the other players too. It had a profound impact on the attitude of the local players.

'Olly was a regular goal scorer but what was really impressive about him, he was composed. Most good strikers around the world, at every level, they slot them in, rather than smash them in. Olly was very good at that. He was confident and could score, I have mental pictures of him slotting it in with the inside of his foot. He was always there following it in, reading the play knowing that if the goalie wasn't going to save it, he would be there to knock it in. Like all good strikers.'

During his playing career, Ollerenshaw also had the opportunity of taking on global giants Manchester United in 1995, joining some Aussies and locals in a Selangor Select XI.

'They asked if Alan Davidson [from Pahang] and I [from Sabah] could come and join their team to make it a bit stronger. That game we had Aussies David Mitchell, Mehmet Durakovic, Josip Biskic, Davo and myself. It was basically five Aussies and six locals.'

Taking on a side that included Eric Cantona and David Beckham in front of 50,000 people at Shah Alam Stadium, Ollerenshaw scored their only goal in a 4–1 defeat. Manchester United used this game as pre-season preparation and would go on to win the English Premier League that season. Ollerenshaw described his goal:

'In the first half, Davo had the ball and Davo being Davo, [he] was screaming at me to make a run, so I made a run and Steve Bruce shoulder-charged me and winded me.

'In the second half, it was almost the same situation, so when Davo had the ball Bruce tried to stop me again but I sidestepped him and went behind him. I was through one- on-one against their goalkeeper Peter Schmeichel and there were these massive arms coming out and I remember thinking don't be a smartarse, just try and hit it as hard as you can, which I did and it went into the corner.

'It's nice to say that you scored against Manchester United.'

A hero in Sabah and nicknamed "the ginger Maradona", Ollerenshaw was recognised everywhere. According to Smith, he was a local celebrity.

'He was a hero in Sabah because he stood out with his ginger mop, and everyone called him Scotty. You couldn't go anywhere locally without people waving at him or yelling *"Scotty"* out of cars!'

Ollerenshaw did not have that same level of recognition when it came to being back home in Australia. He told this story of mistaken identity when it came to Australian sporting celebrities:

'We had just played in the Malaysian Cup Final and it was the last game of the season, and when you've been overseas for nine or ten months, you can't wait to get back to Australia to have a bit of a holiday.

'I was at the airport, flying back to Australia, a couple of days after this game and this guy came up with an Aussie accent and he said, *"I can't believe I'm seeing you here, I've been following your career and you've done so well. This is my son, little Johnny, any chance of an autograph?"* I said *"Sure"* and he gave me a piece of paper and a pen, so I wrote "Little Johnny, Best Regards, Scott Ollerenshaw" and signed it and gave it back to the father.

'He looked at me with this weird look on his face and said, *"Oh sorry mate, I thought you were Mark Woodforde!"*.'

Olly runs a sports tourism business and still lives in Malaysia.

'I came here in '94, and just loved the place. I don't miss out on anything here, I've got satellite TV, I play on a beautiful golf course. There are beautiful resorts, bars, restaurants and food. It's paradise.'

Scott Ollerenshaw | Sabah | 1995

Scott Ollerenshaw's game by game stats for 1995 were unable to be obtained

Scott Ollerenshaw | Sabah | 1996

Scott Ollerenshaw's game by game stats for 1996 were unable to be obtained

Chapter 5
Mark Viduka
Celtic, Scotland, 1999/2000 (25 goals)

'In terms of all-round quality, he's the best male striker Australia has produced. He could hold a ball up if you wanted him to, he could come off and get a turn in, receive at his feet and he could dribble. He had great touch inside.

'Great presence in the box as well, he was the complete striker, he had everything!

'He could still play today in the English Premier League, I reckon.'

John Kosmina's description of Mark Viduka could be somewhat through rose-coloured glasses given Viduka is now in his late 40s, but it shows the high regard that he and most Australian football people had for Viduka's ability.

Viduka is widely regarded as the finest male striker that Australia has produced. Quite the enigma, he has had one of the more outstanding careers that a mere chapter like this cannot do it justice.

Of the top ten most expensive Aussie transfers in history, Mark Viduka features three times. His moves from Dinamo Zagreb to Celtic, Celtic to Leeds, and Leeds to Middlesbrough show his value financially, and indirectly contributed to the building of the Mark Viduka Grandstand at the Somers Street home of the Melbourne Knights.

It was at Celtic that Viduka won his only overseas Golden Boot, scoring 25 goals in the 1999/2000 season. It was quite a tumultuous season. Celtic finished 21 points adrift of title winners (Rangers), saw their main talisman Henrik Larsson injured, and they sacked their manager, John Barnes. Despite all this, Viduka kept on scoring. He won the Golden Boot by six goals.

Viduka's parents met in Melbourne. His mother (a Ukrainian-Croatian migrant) and father (a football-mad Croatian) were involved with Essendon Croatia—also the boyhood club of Eddie Krncevic—this famous football club would soon be known as Melbourne Croatia, and then the Melbourne Knights.

Playing junior football at this club from the age of six, such were Viduka's talents that he would earn a scholarship to the Australian Institute of Sport where he would receive specialised coaching from Ron Smith and former Socceroo Steve O'Connor.

On his return to Melbourne, he would play four games with the Knights in the National Soccer League as a 17-year-old in season 1992/93 scoring two goals.

It's hard to imagine the impact the following two seasons Viduka would have on Australian football through the National Soccer League.

In 1993/94, Viduka scored 17 goals to win the Golden Boot, the Under-21 Player of the Year and the Player of the Year.

He would be selected for the Socceroos in 1994, aged 18, and would debut against South Africa.

Incredibly, Viduka got even better in the following season, netting 21 goals to win another Golden Boot, and back-to-back Under-21 Player of the Year and Player of the Year awards. On top of that, the Melbourne Knights would win their first title when they defeated Adelaide City 2–0 in Adelaide.

The president of the newly independent Croatia, Franjo Tudjman, visited Melbourne in 1995 to implore Viduka to join his club, Dinamo Zagreb. Tudjman was the first democratically elected Croatian president since the Balkan wars and Dinamo Zagreb (then known as Croatia Zagreb) were playing to invoke some national pride within the football community.

It was hard for Viduka to say no, and he would spend the next three seasons playing football in Croatia, winning the League and Cup doubles in each of his three seasons there. When the popularity of Tudjman started to wane, so did the support of Viduka from the club's fans as they were well aware that Viduka was Tudjman's hand-picked star player.

Viduka became exhausted from the Croatian fans and the Croatian press, who were relentless.

He needed a change, and a footballer of his talent had several clubs at the door, but a starring role in a 3–0 Croatia Zagreb defeat of Celtic in the UEFA Cup meant that Celtic knocked the loudest.

He signed to a Celtic team coached by Joe Venglos, known as "Uncle Joe" to Australians ever since he managed the Australian team in 1965 when they unsuccessfully tried to qualify for the World Cup for the first time.

But a mere 36 hours after arriving in Glasgow, Viduka had left Celtic after one training session and returned to Melbourne. After the tribulations of Croatia, he needed a rest.

Football fanzine *Celtic View* wrote several pieces following Viduka's departure questioning whether he was breaching his contract and whether the 'physicals' that club doctors put players through should extend to psychological assessments. They also stated that Celtic offered him the following inducements to stay:

- medical counselling
- a change of hotel
- a furnished apartment
- a car and driver
- an extended Christmas break
- a member of Celtic staff to be with him at all times

Releasing a statement following his departure back to Melbourne, Viduka said:

'It was only after I arrived in Glasgow last week that I started to realise how much I had been affected by events in Zagreb over the last few months where I had been under enormous personal pressure.

'I arrived, ready and wanting to play but it finally became apparent that, having thought a change would be as good as a rest, I realised I actually badly needed a rest.

'It would have been relatively easy for me to cover this up for a few weeks but that would not have been fair on the club, the fans or my family.

'I just hope everyone realises this is not easy for me and appreciates my honesty.

'I realise this is causing great embarrassment and disappointment at the club who have been very supportive and understanding. I would just ask everyone to be patient while I get back to full fitness as soon as possible.'

Michael Gallagher is a lifelong Celtic fan, season ticket holder and an archivist for Glasgow City. He remembers a sense of excitement that they were signing this talent and then not quite understanding why he wasn't playing.

'We didn't have too many foreign signings at that point, but who we did sign were great, so we thought this guy will be the same. He had the pedigree and we wanted to see him play.

'There was a bit of a saga at the start of his time at Celtic and there was a sense that there were dark forces behind the scenes, like scheming player agents or his girlfriend.

'It was not sympathetically handled. No one made any allowances for him.'

The so-called 'Celtic saga' was actually quite short-lived; after departing Glasgow for Melbourne in early December 1998, Viduka was back training with Celtic in late

January 1999. He finished that season playing 11 League and Cup games and scoring eight goals. Celtic fans would have known they had a talent.

Season 1999/2000 now loomed large for Celtic and its supporters. After finishing second to Rangers under Venglos, they appointed a new management dream team of John Barnes and Kenny Dalglish.

Dalglish has long been regarded as the best footballer Scotland has ever produced. He played over 200 times for Celtic before joining Liverpool for more than 300 games, where he was player/manager in his last few seasons.

Barnes was a long-time teammate of Dalglish at Liverpool, however his Celtic appointment was his first professional job as manager.

Leading the line for Celtic that season would be Viduka, the previous season's Golden Boot winner in superstar Swede Henrik Larsson, and former Arsenal and England striker, 37-year-old Ian Wright.

Things started well for Celtic and Viduka. They opened the season with a 5–0 win over Aberdeen with both Viduka and Larsson scoring two each.

Goals against St Johnstone and Hearts were followed up by another double for Viduka against Hibs. In Round 10, Celtic smashed Aberdeen 7–0 with both Viduka and Larsson scoring hattricks, and in the following game Viduka scored a hattrick again, with Ian Wright scoring his first in a 5–1 over Kilmarnock.

Unfortunately for Celtic, Larsson broke his leg in a Champions League match against Lyon and their season went downhill from there. Gallagher recalls it unravelling:

'The Henrik Larsson injury had a lot to do with the Barnes/Dalglish dream team not working. It was bad timing, but crazy looking back on it that Barnes would be the coach and Dalglish would be upstairs looking down and advising him.

'Barnes had no experience at all and he didn't seem to have the temperament for it as well. Some managers come in and have a bit of gravitas, but Barnes it seemed like a friend of a friend recommended him and that connection with Ken was good enough.'

The Larsson injury didn't stop Viduka. He scored in eight games in a row as he took control of goal-scoring duties with his backup Ian Wright sitting on the bench. Despite his form, Celtic were not getting the results they needed to challenge for the title. Draws against Rangers and Kilmarnock followed by a 3–2 loss to Hearts meant that Celtic and Barnes were in the firing line.

A midweek third round Scottish Cup game against Inverness Caledonian Thistle, who were a division below Celtic, proved to be the end of the Barnes/Dalglish dream team.

At halftime in that match Celtic were trailing 2–1 and Viduka was subbed off for Ian Wright. Wright described the halftime situation in his 2016 autobiography, *A Life in Football:*

'Mark Viduka came in at halftime, took his boots off, said *"Fuck this bollocks,"* and refused to go out for the second half. John Barnes was stunned and called him a complete disgrace; Eric Black, who was the assistant manager, called him a fucking disgrace. But he just got up and walked into the shower.'

Inverness Caledonian Thistle ended up winning 3–1 which prompted the famous headline from *The Sun*;

'Super Caley Go Ballistic Celtic Are Atrocious.'

Gallagher wasn't at the game but remembers the sense of inevitability that it would be the end of Barnes' tenure.

'I followed the game on Ceefax, it wasn't on TV. I was at a friend's place, and we were thinking, *"Oh my God we're losing to this lowly team,"* but we also had a sense of relief that Barnes could not survive that loss and it was over.

'A weird kind of happiness after that result, because it just wasn't working for Barnes.'

Dalglish took over from Barnes and three games later, Ian Wright was gone too. After Wright's departure, Viduka scored a brace against St Johnstone to take his season tally to 25. The big number 36 only played in four of the last ten games due to Socceroos' commitments and a couple of minor injuries, but he still won the Golden Boot by six goals.

Another trophy from that season for Viduka was the Scottish Premier League Players' Player of the Year, which he won just ahead of countryman and Socceroos' teammate Craig Moore, then captain of Rangers.

As a team, Celtic were way off—they finished second in the League to Rangers by a whopping 21 points. Gallagher reflected:

'Viduka was the only thing holding the team together that season. And when things don't go so well, the rookie manager gets the blame.'

Celtic would bounce back and Viduka's strike partner Larsson would recover from injury and win the next four Scottish Premier League Golden Boots. It was a partnership gone missing according to Gallagher:

> 'It would have been amazing to see Viduka and Larsson play properly together. You feel that Viduka had a bit of everything—quick, big and strong and skilful, and Larsson could play with anyone, it would have been brilliant.'

Viduka's one season (and a bit) for Celtic would be like some sort of comet. Scouted by Leeds United's Glaswegian-raised Eddie Gray, Viduka would join the English Premier League and spend the next nine seasons in England with Leeds United, Middlesbrough and Newcastle United.

His time in England saw him make the Champions League Semi-Finals, score four goals against Liverpool, and culminate in being named captain of Australia by manager Guus Hiddink for the 2006 World Cup.

His final season for Newcastle United in 2008/09 saw them relegated from the Premier League under Alan Shearer.

Viduka never played professional football again. In typical Viduka fashion, there was no retirement announcement, no send off or testimonial. It was rumoured that he went holidaying on his yacht around Croatia.

His legacy is such that not only is the main grandstand at Melbourne Knights' home ground named after him. Since 2014, the Mark Viduka Medal has been struck to recognise the man of the match in the Australia Cup (formerly the FFA Cup), Australia's premier knockout football competition.

Viduka was also the fourth player recognised by Australia's Professional Football Association with their Alex Tobin Medal. As outlined in Chapter 2, it recognises outstanding attributes: leadership, achievement as a player, commitment to one's fellow professionals, and service and dedication to the game. The three players before him were Joe Marston, Johnny Warren and Craig Johnston.

He is in the Sport Australia Hall of Fame, the Football Australia Hall of Fame and he played 43 times for the Socceroos, scoring 11 goals. Gallagher said of his time at Celtic:

> 'When you look back at the goals Viduka scored that season, they were just ridiculous. He's remembered so fondly at Celtic, because of the whole enigma about him.'

Mark Viduka continues to support the Socceroos and the Australian game from his home in Croatia.

Mark Viduka | Celtic | 1999/2000

Round	H or A	Opposition	Score	Result	Goals
1	H	Aberdeen	0-5	W	2
2	H	St Johnstone	3-0	W	1
3	A	Dundee Utd	2-1	L	0
4	A	Dundee	1-2	W	0
5	H	Hearts	4-0	W	1
6	A	Kilmarnock	0-1	W	Did Not Play
7	A	Hibernian	0-2	W	2
8	H	Aberdeen	7-0	W	3
9	A	St Johnstone	1-2	W	0
10	H	Motherwell	0-1	L	0
11	H	Kilmarnock	5-1	W	3
12	A	Rangers	4-2	L	0
13	A	Hearts	1-2	W	Did Not Play
14	A	Motherwell	3-2	L	1
15	H	Hibernian	4-0	W	1
16	A	Aberdeen	0-6	W	1
17	H	Dundee Utd	4-1	W	1
18	H	Rangers	1-1	D	1
19	A	Kilmarnock	1-1	D	1
20	H	Hearts	2-3	L	1
21	A	Dundee	0-3	W	1
22	H	Dundee	6-2	W	2
23	A	Hibernian	2-1	L	1
24	H	Rangers	0-1	L	0
25	H	St Johnstone	4-1	W	2
26	A	Rangers	4-0	L	0
27	H	Kilmarnock	4-2	W	Did Not Play
28	H	Motherwell	4-0	W	0
29	A	Hearts	0-1	L	Did Not Play
30	H	Dundee	2-2	D	0
31	H	Hibernian	1-1	D	Did Not Play
32	A	Motherwell	1-1	D	0
33	A	Dundee Utd	0-1	W	0
34	H	Aberdeen	5-1	W	Did Not Play
35	A	St Johnstone	0-0	D	Did Not Play
36	H	Dundee Utd	2-0	W	Did Not Play

Chapter 6
Clayton Zane
Lillestrøm, Norway, 2001 (17 goals)

Newcastle and the Hunter Valley region is often seen as the hotbed of Australian football. The coal industry and early football in Australia seemingly went hand in hand as the North East Englishmen and Scots who migrated to Australia to work in the coal mines had a love for the round ball game.

The region has produced some of Australia's most famous footballers: William 'Podge' Maunder, our first ever Socceroos' goal scorer, Reg Date, Alf Quill, Ray Baartz, Col Curran, Craig Johnston and Clayton Zane.

Clayton Zane's name may seem out of place in that list of Newcastle greats, but it's a case of what might have been for the injury-stricken striker.

After a junior career at Cessnock City Hornets and the famous Adamstown Rosebud, Zane made his way into the National Soccer League with local team, Newcastle Breakers. Zane played three seasons with the Breakers, racking up 70 games and 17 goals, before moving to Sydney to join Northern Spirit in 1998.

Northern Spirit was a 'concept' football club in the National Soccer League, drawing on geography rather than any ethnic or historical ties. They had massive early crowds and some big-name players and coaches with returning Socceroos Graham Arnold and Robbie Slater leading the team. Arnold and Slater even became shareholders in the club.

Whilst at Northern Spirit, Zane's personal objective and focus was the 2000 Sydney Olympics. He was desperate to be a part of the Olyroos' team on home soil.

In 1999, he got the chance to progress his career, featuring for the Socceroos against Manchester United at the MCG and Stadium Australia, and in lead-up matches for the Olyroos.

Starting in some unfashionable practice games, Zane featured for the Olyroos against the Port Melbourne Sharks and again against South Korea in Morwell in regional Victoria. With Australia being the host nation of the Olympics, funding allowed for the squad to travel to the UK for some more glamorous ties and the chance to link up with some of their key players who were UK-based—players such as Lucas

Neill and Hayden Foxe—as the Olyroos took on Southampton and Kuwait.

These practice games and the training camp put Zane into the shop window. He had an agent looking out for him, trying to get him a move to Holland or Belgium.

'I got a phone call from my agent saying there is a team up in Norway who are interested in you. So I called Graham Arnold, who was my coach at the time, to tell him and when I rang him he went off his head at me—

"It's a Mickey Mouse league, get your arse home, no need to go up there."

'I wanted to play overseas, so I was prepared to go against his wishes and go and have a look.'

The Norwegian team in question was Molde, a small town with a population of around 30,000, based in the northwest of the country. The football club was owned by Kjell Inge Røkke, an oil magnate who was one of the richest men in the country. Not much was known about the Scandinavian Leagues back then. However in 1999, Molde was in the Champions League.

This news resulted in a change of tune from Zane's NSL manager Graham Arnold.

'Arnie called me back and said, *"Listen I think this could be a really good move for you."*'

Zane went to Molde to find out more, but he was a little underwhelmed with the small town. As Molde were preparing for a Champions League group game with Real Madrid, they invited him to play in a training match. Scoring three goals in the trial, Molde was keen to sign Zane and have him stay to watch the game against Real Madrid. But Zane wanted to head back to Australia.

'I had to get back to Northern Spirit. They [Molde] wanted to sign me straight away and the transfer fee at the time was massive for the club, I don't think anyone [at Spirit] realised they [Molde] had that much money.'

The small Norwegian town didn't impress Zane, despite the beautiful scenery and mountains. The main street only had a couple of shops, and they were a seven-hour drive away from the capital city, Oslo. He was prepared to knuckle down for Northern Spirit and focus on the upcoming Olympics, but Molde was persistent in getting their man.

'I didn't want to go to Norway when I got back to Northern Spirit, because it was such a small town and having been up there for a week I didn't know if I could live there.

'They came back three times; twice I said no, and in the end they called me back and the owner said, *"If you don't say yes this time he's going to fly out on his private jet and pick you up and bring you back anyway so I suggest you say yes to it."'*

Molde's persistence was also shown with the money on offer. The transfer fee at the time was $A700,000, good money in 1999 and at the time the second highest fee for a player coming directly from the NSL behind goalkeeper Zeljko Kalac. With player/ manager Graham Arnold also being a shareholder in the Spirit, it was an offer too good to refuse. As Zane put it:

'When someone comes back a second or third time, you know they really want you.'

With the Olympics pending, Zane arranged with Molde that he would be available for anything Olyroo-related, even in-season, as he didn't want to be out of sight and out of mind when it came to the Olympic selectors. The arrangement allowed him to leave Norway for training camps and games, and during his season at Molde, he left for Australia four times.

'It disturbed my season massively which they knew at the time. I didn't want to miss out, I wanted to make the Olympics. That was the agreement we had written into my contract. I could go at any time that was required.'

Molde didn't have a great season. They finished seventh in the League and Zane never started, making 14 appearances off the bench. He was often played out of position, more as a midfielder than a striker. He just couldn't find enough form to get into the team and when he would get close, he was off back to Australia.

It wasn't all doom and gloom though—Zane became an Olympian and played for the Olyroos, featuring in the games against Nigeria and Honduras. But it was a disappointing tournament for the hosts, losing all three group games.

With Zane's second season at Molde approaching, he was preparing to work hard in pre-season to push his case:

'I thought the next year would be like my first, where I would try and get in the first team, but the new coach came in and he looked at the squad and he pulled me aside and said maybe start looking for another club as he wanted to build a new team.'

With the club deep into pre-season, Zane's agent was looking for another team, but it was getting harder to find somewhere. Then a chance pre-season friendly in Molde turned his fortunes around. Molde was hosting Lillestrøm SK and Zane was having a team lunch at one of the two hotels in the town when his phone rang.

'I got a phone call from my agent saying he needed to talk to me urgently, he said Lillestrøm wanted to take me on loan.

'He asked if I wanted to do it and then he talked me into it. He said it's for one month and if you're not going to play at Molde, you might as well go.'

In an awkward situation, Zane said his goodbyes and walked across the road to the other hotel in Molde to join Lillestrøm SK, who were there having a team lunch ahead of the friendly.

'I had already eaten, I just walked in and sat there. I didn't know anyone. Then at the ground, most of the people at the club didn't know what was going on and then for the game, I was on the opposition bench. I was really embarrassed. I came on in that game and played the last 20 minutes and everyone at Molde cheered me on and wished me well.'

At the start of his second Norwegian season, Zane was on the bench for Lillestrøm SK's first game of the season and he didn't get a run. In his second match, he was brought on at halftime, played well, and was in the starting 11 from then on.

The change of scenery would prove to be a turning point in Zane's football, helping his mental health and really turning it around on the pitch.

'It's not until I arrived at Molde and unpacked my bags that I realised how lonely it would be. Coming from Sydney at the time, it was a noticeable difference. It was starting to get cold there and I was worried that I wouldn't be able to handle living there.

'Moving was a game changer, it was one of the things I really needed. I felt like I was the only foreigner in Molde and with Lillestrøm SK I was living in Oslo. It's only 20 minutes to Lillestrøm and you could catch a train to Oslo if you didn't want to drive.'

The brotherhood of Aussie footballers was also alive and well with a fair few Aussies also in Norway at the time.

'Kasey Werhman was there, Stephen Laybutt came to play up there. Michael Petkovic, the goalkeeper, came up to Lillestrøm on loan, [and] the whole move just felt more comfortable.'

However, Zane's 2001 season was disrupted as he joined the Socceroos for the Confederations Cup held in South Korea and Japan, a tournament that would see the Australians defeat both France and Brazil in finishing third. He famously scored the only goal in a 1–0 win over reigning world and European Cup champions, France.

It proved to be the finest season of Clayton Zane's career—Lillestrøm SK finished runners-up in the League and Zane scored 17 goals from only 19 appearances. He joined Thorstein Helstad from Brann and Frode Johnsen from Rosenborg in a three-way tie for the Golden Boot. What made Zane's achievement even more noticeable is that he was the first non-Norwegian to win a scoring title, and out of the three winners, he was the only player not to take any penalty kicks.

'I played a few games less than Helstad and Johnsen and I never took any penalties. I regret it now. We had a guy called Tourias Hansen, a defender, a left back, I think he scored nine goals that year, all penalties! He scored and then he just kept scoring so it never opened for me to take a penalty.

'I punched above my weight though; I mean [from] 14 sub appearances the year before to surprising everyone with a Golden Boot.'

According to Zane, Lillestrøm SK also played above themselves that season in coming second.

'We had good team spirit; the coach was old school, playing 4–4–2, and we were a physical team. Everything about it suited me, a real family club, we exceeded expectations, and the season came down to the last game. We needed to win and we needed Rosenberg to drop points. We did the right thing and won 3–1 against Tromso, but unfortunately for us, Rosenberg won their match.

'It was a good time, I really hit my straps [due to] my confidence from the Olympics [and] getting involved with the senior Socceroos and [I] was just getting started, but injury killed me really young.'

From the highs of that magnificent year at Lillestrøm, Zane was sold to Anderlecht in Belgium on a four-year deal for a then club record of two million Euros.

Anderlecht is the club where Eddie Krncevic started these Golden Boot stories, but severe knee injuries curtailed Zane's career. He only managed 10 games and two goals in four seasons in Belgium. Zane summed up his four frustrating years there:

'The coach who signed me at Anderlecht got moved to the national team. He signed me and then left, so when I turned up to my first training session the new coach didn't know who I was, so I thought, *"Here we go again."* I was on the bench for the first game and then I came off the bench in the second game away from home and scored in a 2–0 win.

'I started quite well and then a couple of games in I started to feel pain. I could hardly walk, and I hadn't felt anything during the game and then everything just snowballed from there.

'I got a knee injury, the cartilage behind my kneecap, the articular cartilage. I think today with sports science you could probably still play, but then, once you damage that, it's hard. I had a kind of surgery, which they don't do anymore, where they take cartilage out of your knee, then they regrow it in a laboratory and then they sew it back in where it was damaged.

'Every time I tried to come back from it, I just kept breaking down, I was always in pain and it became a bit of a mental struggle to try and come back from it.

'I was 24 years old when I got injured. I had a four-year contract there and I just sat the contract out, trying to come back and then I went back to Norway for a couple of years with manager Henning Berg with a team called Lyn. I tried to get back into the shop window there, but after the trial I just said *"I'm done"*—I just knew it. I didn't want to waste my time or their money.

'Basically the insurance just paid Anderlecht. I went from age 24 to 28 contracted to Anderlecht trying to come back from injury, it was a nightmare!'

Despite the injury curse, Clayton Zane is a Socceroo, an Olympian and one of only 12 Australians to win a Golden Boot overseas, something he and his family can be immensely proud of.

'I'm not too nostalgic, but at the time when I do think back, I was in good form, I had just broken into the Socceroos and ended up playing 14 games, which is a highlight playing for your country.

'I would have liked to see where I could have gone. My positioning and my timing were coming together and I wasn't at the peak age for a footballer when I finished.'

Despite his body letting him down, Zane was not lost to the game as he moved into coaching and management, working with junior teams with Queens Park Rangers in England before heading back home to work with the Newcastle Jets in the A-League.

He has managed the senior women's, men's and youth teams at the Jets as well as working as an assistant coach to Mark Jones, Ernie Merrick, Carl Robinson, Craig Deans and Arthur Pappas. He still runs his own personal football coaching service in Newcastle called InZane Football.

Clayton Zane | Lillestrøm | 2001

Round	H or A	Opposition	Score	Result	Goals
1	H	Bryne FK	0-0	D	Did Not Play
2	A	Strømsgodset	1-2	W	0
3	H	Sogndal IL	4-1	W	0
4	A	Odd Grenland	4-1	L	0
5	H	Lyn FK	2-1	W	2
6	H	Bodø/Glimt	1-0	W	1
7	A	Stabæk Fotball	3-2	L	1
8	H	Brann	2-1	W	2
9	A	Viking FK	3-2	L	1
10	H	Molde	4-1	W	Did Not Play
11	A	Rosenborg	2-2	D	Did Not Play
12	H	Moss FK	3-0	W	Did Not Play
13	A	Tromsø IL	0-3	W	1
14	A	Bryne FK	0-5	W	2
15	H	Strømsgodset	7-4	W	1
16	A	Sogndal IL	2-2	D	1
17	H	Odd Grenland	3-3	D	1
18	A	Lyn FK	0-2	W	1
19	A	Bodø/Glimt	1-2	W	0
20	H	Stabæk Fotball	2-1	W	0
21	A	Brann	1-1	D	0
22	H	Viking FK	4-0	W	2
23	A	Molde	1-2	W	0
24	H	Rosenborg	1-2	L	0
25	A	Moss FK	0-2	W	0
26	H	Tromsø IL	3-1	W	1

Chapter 7
Scott McDonald
Celtic, Scotland, 2007/08 (25 goals)

Scott McDonald was born in Melbourne to Scottish parents. Both of his parents hailed from Glasgow but met in Australia at the local football club. McDonald's mother's family were all Rangers' fans and McDonald's father's family were all Celtic fans.

McDonald was, and still is, a Celtic fan.

One of the youngest ever players to debut in Australia's national League, McDonald burst onto the scene as a 15-year-old, playing three games off the bench with Morwell (Gippsland) Falcons in the National Soccer League. This led to his selection in the Under-17 Australian team. He featured prominently in the 'Joeys' squad that made the 1999 Under- 17 World Cup Final in New Zealand.

It certainly put McDonald in the shop window and having a UK passport through his parents helped propel him towards a next step in Europe.

'I scored a couple of goals and had played well. There were a lot of scouts there and because our team made the Final, we had a bit of attention.'

There was talk of McDonald heading to Germany or even an early move to Celtic, but it was Southampton in England who came to him with a formal contract. McDonald and his father visited the Premier League club for a week and he made the decision to join the Saints.

'As my Dad said at the time, it is too good an opportunity to turn down. If you don't do it, you will regret it [for] the rest of your life. At that time there was nowhere to go to in Australia other than the AIS, I was 50/50 on it. When you are a kid, you don't really want to leave your friends and family.'

McDonald would join Southampton and toiled away for a few years (including loan stints with Huddersfield Town and AFC Bournemouth), eventually working his way up to make his debut in the Premier League. He seemed to be working his way through top-flight football, but a managerial change brought things to a close.

'Gordon Strachan came in as a new manager and he had different opinions on selection. We were looking at survival in the Premier League, so more experienced players are selected and you find yourself on the outer. You don't really know how to cope with the disappointment of not starting and building up from the beginning.'

Strachan would become a big part of McDonald's career in the UK, even if their initial relationship didn't start so smoothly at Southampton.

After Southampton, McDonald had a month-to-month rolling contract at Wimbledon, but that wasn't working well either. Eventually it was Scotland that would end up giving McDonald the chance to showcase his talents.

Not at his beloved Celtic though! Former England captain Terry Butcher, just before his stint at the helm of Sydney FC, was the manager at Motherwell and he would give McDonald the chance to show his wares 20 kilometres away from Celtic Park.

A slow start for McDonald at Motherwell saw him only score one goal in 2003/04, his debut season. Things certainly changed the following season as he stamped his arrival in Scotland with 15 goals for the season, leading the goal scoring for Motherwell and finishing sixth overall in the Scottish Premiership's Golden Boot, but it was his 14th and 15th goals for Motherwell that etched him into Celtic folklore—for all the wrong reasons for Celtic fans.

Going into the final round of the 2004/05 season, Celtic were two points clear of arch-rival Rangers. Rangers had a tough match against third-placed Hibs at Easter Road, whilst Celtic took on McDonald's Motherwell, then in seventh place, at their home ground, Fir Park.

Rangers defeated Hibs 1–0 and Celtic were clinging to a 1–0 lead before McDonald equalised in the 88th minute with an incredible over the shoulder effort. Then in the 90th minute, he scored Motherwell's winner via a deflection. In what became known as "Helicopter Sunday", lifelong Celtic fan McDonald ensured Celtic missed out and their Old Firm rivals won the title. It is something that follows McDonald everywhere he goes.

'The repercussions of that will always be there and remembered…I mean if I had a pound for every time someone mentions that to me. Even last week I had a Rangers fan come up to me and say it was one of the best days of his life.

'I always get, *"You gave me one of the worst days"* or *"You gave me one of the best days"* and I get that quite regularly. That's the way it is but it also propelled my football career.'

Despite playing for Motherwell, the Celtic connection with the McDonald family never faltered, even after "Helicopter Sunday".

'My grandfather was at the Celtic supporter's club in Melbourne and had to get escorted out!

'I also got tickets for my now father-in-law, who is a Celtic tragic. He was at the game with his three brothers and after the game I was flying back to Southampton to meet my now wife to go on holiday. He was up at one end of the plane and I was at the other, he just couldn't look at me.'

The next two seasons at Motherwell further cemented McDonald's credentials with 11 goals in 2005/06 and 13 in 2006/07. Gordon Strachan, the manager who let McDonald go from Southampton, came after McDonald when he arrived at Celtic and the conversation was a quick one.

'Gordon had seen a change in me, a humility and how I worked with my team. The conversation went, *"Do you have a problem working with me?"* and I was like, *"Absolutely not."* So he said, *"Right, then get the contract signed and let's go."*'

Before signing with Celtic, McDonald was with the national team preparing for the 2007 Asian Cup and had the chance to discuss the move with former Hoops striker, Mark Viduka.

'When I was about to sign at Celtic I was in China with the Socceroos and it was one of Mark's last games before the Asian Cup. One of the first people I asked was Mark and he was like, *"God mate, go. They are a great club. Good luck to you!"* Someone that I looked up to as an Australian who played for Celtic, it was great to get his blessing.'

McDonald signing for Celtic might have been a boyhood dream come true for him, but it was going to take a whole lot more to win over the Celtic fans.

Celtic season ticket-holder and Glasgow City archivist Michael Gallagher remembers it well:

'His backstory meant there wasn't a lot of goodwill when he signed. He had a lot of catching up to do after giving Rangers the title!

'He was signed by Gordon Strachan who was manager, and a lot of the signings felt quite belligerent as he signed a couple of guys who were at Rangers, like Steven Pressley and a goalkeeper Mark Brown. It was like he was sticking two fingers up to the fans almost.

'Scott McDonald fitted into that signing model of Strachan, an old-school manager who didn't care what anybody thought of him.'

They tried to push the Celtic background angle when McDonald arrived, focusing on his family connection and that he was a childhood fan. The fanzines ran with pics of him as a kid in a Celtic top.

Despite the initial scepticism, McDonald's debut season for Celtic reached incredible heights. He started well and he never looked back, scoring in the Champions League, getting back-to-back home ground hattricks, as well as doubles against Aberdeen and Rangers.

'I debuted in the Champions League. In my first game, I set up the goal against Spartak. It settled my nerves, and my confidence grew from that moment, and the next leg I scored my first ever goal for Celtic against Spartak Moscow to qualify for the Champions League, and then on the weekend after I got my first goal in the League against St Mirren.'

It could have been quite different. The League game against Aberdeen was played between the Spartak Moscow Champions League games and McDonald was benched with the score at 1–1. His replacement Kenny Miller scored twice to give Celtic the win. Strachan saw something in McDonald and helped his frame of mind by starting him the game after.

'Gordon put me straight in and your confidence lifts from there when the manager believes in you. Then I got the nod for the first game against Aberdeen and within the first ten minutes I missed a glorious chance from a glancing header that just went wide. I ended up not scoring that game and we were drawing 1–1, and then Kenny replaces me and scores a double. So you're sat there thinking, *"It's great we won, but I'm going to be spending a wee while on the bench."'*

McDonald's goal against St Mirren was followed up three weeks later with back-to-back hattricks at home in a 3–0 win over Dundee United and a 3–0 win over his old side Motherwell. And from there he was on a roll.

'I didn't look back, I really didn't, my confidence lifted, and I kept working hard at training. Gordon was big on forward play at training, plenty of repetitive stuff but then it would all become an unconscious state where goal scoring is just natural and you just do it, because you have just done it time and again at training.'

If being a centre-forward is a confidence game, then McDonald had it in spades that season.

'I was going into games going, *"I know I am going to score today, but I am playing for Celtic, so how many am I scoring?"*
'There is a lot to be said about mentality, the psychological side of football. Confidence within the game—at that point I felt invincible. Whether it was St Mirren, or Motherwell or AC Milan in the Champions League at Celtic Park and you always knew you were a chance when you played for Celtic, so you just had to be ready.'

McDonald gained a sense of superpowers when he donned the green and white hoops of Celtic, knowing that nearly every season they would have one of the strongest squads in the Scottish Premiership. He figured that if he could score goals for Motherwell, then scoring for Celtic should be easier and he should be scoring more.

'At Motherwell, there was a heavy reliance on making things happen myself, I had to work harder. What I worked out early at Celtic is that I had such good players around me I just had to do the simple things well, get in the right areas and just be in the danger zone.
'So as soon as he gets it, I know where I am going, I am going straight for the six-yard box, and I became this sort of poacher at Celtic. Realistically that role

wasn't me, but it was the type of player I became, because I knew it was what I had to do playing for Celtic.'

Yet it was that poacher role in which Australia unsuccessfully tried to play McDonald. He was played out of position in the national team, infamously never scoring in 26 Socceroos' games. With aerial threats in the national team coming from players such as Viduka, Josh Kennedy and Tim Cahill, McDonald rarely got an opportunity to impress or play his natural game with the Socceroos.

Despite being Australia's Overseas Player of the Year in 2008 and having three consecutive seasons of ten or more goals in the Scottish Premiership, he failed to make the Socceroos' 2010 World Cup squad. Richard Garcia was played as the lone striker against Germany in the first game at the 2010 World Cup in South Africa, and McDonald was not even in the country.

'With Australia, I was always second guessing what would happen. But at Celtic I didn't have to, I just knew.'

McDonald credited Strachan and his training methods for ensuring he was always in the right place. Repetition and running to the right spots is something McDonald is trying to bring into the next phase of his career in coaching on the Gold Coast.

'Through Gordon's training, you kept getting better. So, when it came to a Saturday, you were in the right positions. The feeling in those first few seasons at Celtic was that you were invincible. You felt you could take it out of the sky and hit one from 25 yards on the volley and it would go in the top corner at training.

'When you have that confidence and the manager has taught you to know where the ball is going to be, then you understand the telepathy with the players that are playing with you that you know what the players are going to do, you will attack it and you will gamble 100 times more than if you were playing with players that you don't quite know.'

McDonald helped clinch Celtic the title in wonderful fashion by defeating Rangers at home with three games to go in the season. He scored two goals and won a penalty in the 70th minute for Celtic to clinch the title. Barry Robson scored from the penalty to secure the title for Celtic. McDonald was denied a hattrick due to missing a penalty the game before.

Three weeks later at the end of the season, McDonald had won the Golden Boot with 25 goals, ten clear of his nearest rival, Celtic teammate Jan Vennegoor of Hesselink. He said:

'That's what you contribute for, to win things. When you win something and you score so many goals that season, it is an honour to be a part of.'

McDonald continued to win things, securing the title with Celtic the following season (2008/09) when he finished second to Rangers' Kris Boyd in the Golden Boot award, scoring 16 goals. Despite finishing second, McDonald felt he was a better player in his second season with Celtic.

'Most of that season, I played without a partner and had a lot more attention from the opposition, but I helped out more creating opportunities for others and improving in the game.'

He had a third and final season with Celtic, scoring ten goals as they finished runners-up to Rangers for the 2009/10 title.

A prolific three seasons at Celtic ended with McDonald following Gordon Strachan back to England as he took on the manager's role at Middlesbrough.

'I sometimes wish I never left, that's how much Celtic means to me, and how much I missed it. It took me a long time to get over it, and it was hard going back to watching Celtic again rather than being a part of it.'

'In that time, Gordon was a real fatherly figure to me and was a major influence in me going there. I would never have gone to Middlesbrough at that point without Gordon's influence and leaving Celtic, a club I loved. The relationship with him is still strong to this day. I've known Gordon [for] a really long time now.'

After over 100 games at Middlesbrough, McDonald then played with Millwall before a return to Scotland saw further games at Motherwell and Dundee United. He worked briefly as a pundit for the BBC before coming out of retirement to help Partick Thistle avoid relegation in the Scottish Championship.

McDonald returned to Australia for a couple of seasons in the A-League, playing for Western United, Brisbane Roar and Western Sydney Wanderers. His is the longest Australian men's national League career between his first game (at the Falcons in season 1998/99) and his last (with the Wanderers in season 2020/21), spanning well over 20 years.

He is now combining coaching and media work, leading the Gold Coast Knights in Queensland's National Premier League competition, as well as making television appearances on Champions League coverage in Australia.

In 2023, Gold Coast Knights nominated to compete in the national second-tier competition.

Scott McDonald | Celtic | 2007/08

Round	H or A	Opposition	Score	Result	Goals
1	H	Kilmarnock	0-0	D	Did Not Play
2	A	Falkirk	1-4	W	Did Not Play
3	A	Aberdeen	1-3	W	0
4	H	Hearts	5-0	W	0
5	A	St Mirren	1-5	W	1
6	H	Inverness CT	5-0	W	0
7	A	Hibernian	3-2	L	0
8	H	Dundee Utd	3-0	W	3
9	A	Gretna FC	1-2	W	1
10	A	Rangers	3-0	L	0
11	H	Motherwell	3-0	W	3
12	A	Kilmarnock	1-2	W	2
13	H	Falkirk	4-0	W	1
14	H	Aberdeen	3-0	W	1
15	A	Hearts	1-1	D	1
16	H	St Mirren	1-1	D	0
17	A	Inverness CT	3-2	L	0
18	H	Hibernian	1-1	D	0
19	A	Dundee Utd	0-2	W	0
20	H	Gretna FC	3-0	W	1
21	H	Rangers	2-1	W	0
22	A	Motherwell	1-4	W	1
23	H	Kilmarnock	1-0	W	0
24	A	Falkirk	0-1	W	1
25	A	Aberdeen	1-5	W	2
26	H	Hearts	3-0	W	1
27	A	St Mirren	0-1	W	0
28	H	Inverness CT	2-1	W	1
29	A	Hibernian	0-2	W	0
30	H	Dundee Utd	0-0	D	0
31	A	Gretna FC	0-3	W	1
32	A	Rangers	1-0	L	0
33	H	Motherwell	0-1	L	0
34	H	Aberdeen	1-0	W	0
35	H	Rangers	3-2	W	2
36	A	Motherwell	1-2	W	1
37	H	Hibernian	2-0	W	1
38	A	Dundee Utd	0-1	W	0

Chapter 8
Josh Kennedy
Nagoya Grampus, Japan, 2010
(17 goals)
Nagoya Grampus, Japan, 2011
(19 goals)

Melbourne rock band Jet rocketed to fame in 2001 when their single *Are You Gonna Be My Girl* formed part of two major worldwide advertising campaigns for both Vodafone and the Apple iPod.

Eight years later, the lead single from their third album was *She's a Genius!*. Little did the band know that Japanese supporters of the Nagoya Grampus football club would adopt that song as the anthem for their Australian striker, Josh Kennedy.

She's a Genius! became "He's a Jesus!" to the fans as Kennedy's back-to-back Golden Boot seasons of 2010 and 2011 helped Nagoya Grampus experience their best era in the J1 League, culminating in their one and only title in 2010.

Kennedy was born in Wodonga and grew up in the country town of Yackandandah along the Victoria–New South Wales border. A natural striker, his junior prowess was such that he played alongside Scott McDonald in the Australian Under-17 team (the Joeys) who played in the 1999 World Cup in New Zealand.

This led to a stint at the Australian Institute of Sport and a four-game spell in 1999 with short-lived National Soccer League club, Carlton.

Following his work with the Joeys, the AIS and in the NSL, Kennedy's potential saw him signed by German club VFL Wolfsburg to begin a career that would see him play for six German clubs, feature in two World Cups, and have success in Japan before returning to club football in Australia.

The 194-centimetre Kennedy made his debut in the Bundesliga at only 17 and first scored in that competition aged just 18. However, being so young and stifled for opportunities, he would move to the third-tier Stuttgart Kickers for a spell before establishing himself with Dynamo Dresden in Bundesliga 2.

Despite spending five years in Europe following his AIS stint, when Guus Hiddink selected Kennedy for the 2006 World Cup squad, it seemed as if he was being plucked from obscurity as an uncapped player.

However, three goals on debut for Australia against club side, VV Kloetinge, followed by a goal in his first full Socceroos' A international against Liechtenstein soon had the Australian public thinking they had an 'X factor' in their tall centre-forward.

Quickly nicknamed "Jesus" due to his resemblance to the traditional depiction of Christ with his long hair, beard and headband, Kennedy's second and third Socceroos' games were in the 2006 World Cup against Japan and Croatia.

A return to the top-flight competition in Germany beckoned soon after when he signed with FC Nürnburg, but an Achilles tendon rupture in his first training session there halted his football action and would prove to be the start of an injury-interrupted career. After 12 games and one goal at FC Nürnberg, he moved to Karlsruher SC for 33 games.

When Karlsruher SC were relegated following the 2008/09 season, Kennedy moved to Japan and benefitted directly from Australia's move from Oceania into the Asian Football Confederation (AFC).

The J1 League had a rule that all clubs were allowed three foreign players and one foreign player from within the Asian Football Confederation. Most Japanese clubs used their AFC spot with a South Korean, but Kennedy proved to be the exception. In 2010, he was one of only two non-Koreans being used by clubs in their AFC spot. He joined Nagoya Grampus, the original football club of car manufacturing giant, Toyota.

Kazane Kuwahara is a long-time season-ticket holder of Nagoya Grampus. He grew up in Nagoya and his mother was the club interpreter when Arsene Wenger was their manager in 1995, before he joined Arsenal in the English Premier League and took all before him. He recalled the recruitment of Kennedy in that AFC position:

'Having an Australian was unique, but it was the right decision. Most Japanese fans think that Korean players get angry quickly. We had a Korean before Josh who was a very good player, but he was very rough and would often get angry and get cards, so he was difficult to manage. Josh was a welcome change.'

Kennedy started with Nagoya Grampus in 2009 but it was the 2010 season when both he and Nagoya announced their arrival on the J1 League scene.

Starting with a goal and an assist against Gamba Osaka, Kennedy was a model of consistency, scoring in 15 games of the 34-match season with doubles against Vegalta Sendai and Shimizu S-Pulse.

With 23 wins and three draws, Nagoya Grampus won their first and so far only title in the J1 League, finishing ten points clear on top of the tree. Led by former player Dragan Stojković who was voted Coach of the Year, the J1 League team of the season comprised five Nagoya Grampus players including Kennedy. Kuwahara reflected:

'That was without doubt the best season in our history, the first and only time we won the League. Our head coach Dragan Stojković was a former player, he is still the best- scoring player in our history.

'He came back to Nagoya Grampus as manager in 2008 and made us the champions in 2010.

'We were so strong that year with Josh Kennedy and other Japanese national players.'

Kennedy shared the Golden Boot that season with Ryoichi Maeda of Jubilo Iwata, both scoring 17 goals. His high-profile Japanese teammate Keiji Tamada scored 13 for Nagoya Grampus.

Prior to that season, Tamada had shared the pitch with Kennedy at the World Cup in 2006 when the Blue Samurai played the Socceroos.

In 2011, Nagoya Grampus had higher hopes for the season and were pushing for back-to-back titles. Despite Kennedy and Tamada having better seasons, Nagoya Grampus would finish the season second by one point to Kashiwa Reysol. The Nagoya Grampus fans continued with their Jet-inspired chant for Kennedy. According to Kuwahara, it was something he embraced and got involved with as well—

'Before the game, [we] would start that chant during the warm-up session. We would sing a song for each player, and whenever we sang for Josh, he would stop training and clap along with us.

'We loved him and we still love Josh so much!'

Kennedy would follow up his title-winning Golden Boot season of 2010 with a consecutive Golden Boot in 2011, this time with 19 goals. He was at the peak of his powers.

However, injuries and playing injured curtailed Kennedy's remaining three seasons in Japan. After playing more than 30 games a season in 2010 and 2011, he could only manage 11 games and five goals in 2014. That season saw Nagoya Grampus relegated to J2. From the highs of winning the title, four seasons later they went down. Kuwahara puts it down to an injured Kennedy.

'Because of Josh's injury, our scoring got worse. It was the reason for our downfall in 2014 and relegation to J2. He was so important for us.

'At the same time Kennedy scored against Iraq to take Australia to the World Cup, the Nagoya Grampus fans were watching the game and got so excited to see him score, even if he was struggling with injury.'

Kennedy replaced Tim Cahill off the bench in that final World Cup Qualifier against Iraq in Sydney to qualify for the 2014 World Cup in Brazil. In the 83rd minute, six minutes after coming off the bench, he scored with a header to take Australia to its third consecutive World Cup. His celebration seemed to mimic Rio's Christ the Redeemer statue and most media outlets played up to that with his previous nickname of "Jesus", with headlines such as "Jesus Saves". Unfortunately, injury prevented him joining the Socceroos for their third consecutive World Cup in Brazil.

Over 40 Australians have played professionally in the J1 League and with two Golden Boots to his name, Kennedy is the most influential of all those who have played there so far.

Post Japan, Kennedy returned with his family to Melbourne and to the A-League with Melbourne City as the club's Australian marquee player. Injuries again curtailed his return, and despite signing for two years he appeared only 14 times, scoring twice—one of those was a winning goal in New Zealand in a knockout Final against Wellington Phoenix.

Once back in Melbourne, his wife Jacinta, a former member of the Australian national basketball team (the Opals), whom he had met at the AIS as a teenager (and who had stopped her basketball career to start their family), returned to the Women's National Basketball League to play with her former club the Dandenong Rangers after an absence of nine years.

John Kosmina summed up the career of Kennedy:

'Injuries curtailed what Josh could have achieved. I thought he was a tall, thin version of Mark Viduka.

'He had great touch, was really good in the air, and for a big guy, he had great feet.

'He did well in Germany, but Japanese football suited him because he was so tall and they used his height to [their] advantage.

'He always got into great positions, and he could finish. He was a fantastic footballer and probably never got the recognition he deserved. He is a real nice character as well and cool under pressure.'

Josh Kennedy continues to work in the game in Australia with professional roles at both Football Victoria and Football Australia.

Josh Kennedy | Nagoya Grampus | 2010

Round	H or A	Opposition	Score	Result	Goals
1	A	Gamba Osaka	1-2	W	1
2	H	Kawasaki Frontale	2-3	L	0
3	H	Jubilo Iwata	2-0	W	1
4	A	Sanfreece Hiroshima	0-1	L	Did Not Play
5	H	Vissel Kobe	2-0	W	0
6	A	Kyota Sanga	0-2	W	1
7	H	Albirex Niigata	1-1	D	0
8	A	Cerezo Osaka	0-1	W	Did Not Play
9	H	Monte Yamagata	2-1	W	1
10	A	Urawa Reds	2-1	L	1
11	A	Vegalta Sendai	1-2	W	2
12	H	Kashima Antlers	1-4	L	1
13	A	Omiya Ardija	0-1	W	1
14	H	Shimizu S-Pulse	3-3	D	0
15	H	Shonan Belmare	2-1	W	0
16	A	Yokohama F Marinos	0-2	W	1
17	A	FC Tokyo	0-1	W	0
18	H	Urawa Reds	3-1	W	0
19	A	Kawasaki Frontale	4-0	L	0
20	H	Gamba Osaka	3-1	W	1
21	H	Kyoto Sanga	1-0	W	0
22	A	Monte Yamagata	0-1	W	0
23	H	Yokohama F Marinos	1-1	D	0
24	A	Shimizu S-Pulse	1-5	W	2
25	H	Vegalta Dendai	2-1	W	1
26	A	Albirex Niigata	4-1	L	1
27	A	Vissel Kobe	1-2	W	0
28	H	Cerezo Osaka	1-0	W	1
29	A	Kashima Antlers	1-0	L	0
30	H	Omiya Ardija	2-1	W	Did Not Play
31	A	Shonan Belmare	0-1	W	0
32	H	FC Tokyo	0-1	L	0
33	A	Jubilo Iwata	1-2	W	0
34	H	Sanfreece Hiroshima	2-1	W	1

Josh Kennedy | Nagoya Grampus | 2011

Round	H or A	Opposition	Score	Result	Goals
1	H	Yokohama F Marinos	1-1	D	1
2	A	Velgata Sendai	1-0	L	0
3	A	Vissel Kobe	0-1	W	0
4	H	Kasima Antlers	2-1	W	1
5	A	Monte Yamagata	0-2	W	1
6	H	Sanfreece Hiroshima	3-2	W	0
7	A	Urawa Reds	3-0	L	0
8	H	Kawasaki Frontale	2-0	W	0
9	A	Gamba Osaka	2-2	D	1
10	H	Shimizu S-Pulse	1-1	D	Did Not Play
11	A	Ventforet Kofu	3-1	L	Did Not Play
12	H	Kashiwa Reysol	0-0	D	Did Not Play
13	H	Avispa Fukuoka	5-2	W	1
14	A	Jubilo Iwata	0-1	W	0
15	H	Albirex Niigata	4-0	W	2
16	H	Omiya Ardija	2-2	D	1
17	A	Cerezo Osaka	2-3	W	1
18	H	Urawa Reds	1-1	D	0
19	A	Avispa Fukuoka	0-3	W	1
20	H	Jubilo Iwata	2-1	W	0
21	A	Sanfreece Hiroshima	0-3	W	1
22	H	Velgata Sendai	0-1	L	0
23	A	Kawasaki Frontale	1-2	W	2
24	H	Ventforet Kofu	4-1	W	1
25	A	Kashiwa Reysol	2-1	L	0
26	A	Kashima Antlers	1-1	D	0
27	H	Vissel Kobe	3-1	W	1
28	A	Shimizu S-Pulse	2-0	L	0
29	H	Gamba Osaka	4-1	W	0
30	A	Omiya Ardija	2-3	W	1
31	H	Cerezo Osaka	3-1	W	1
32	A	Yokahama F Marinos	1-2	W	1
33	H	Monte Yamagata	3-0	W	1
34	A	Albirex Niigata	0-1	W	0

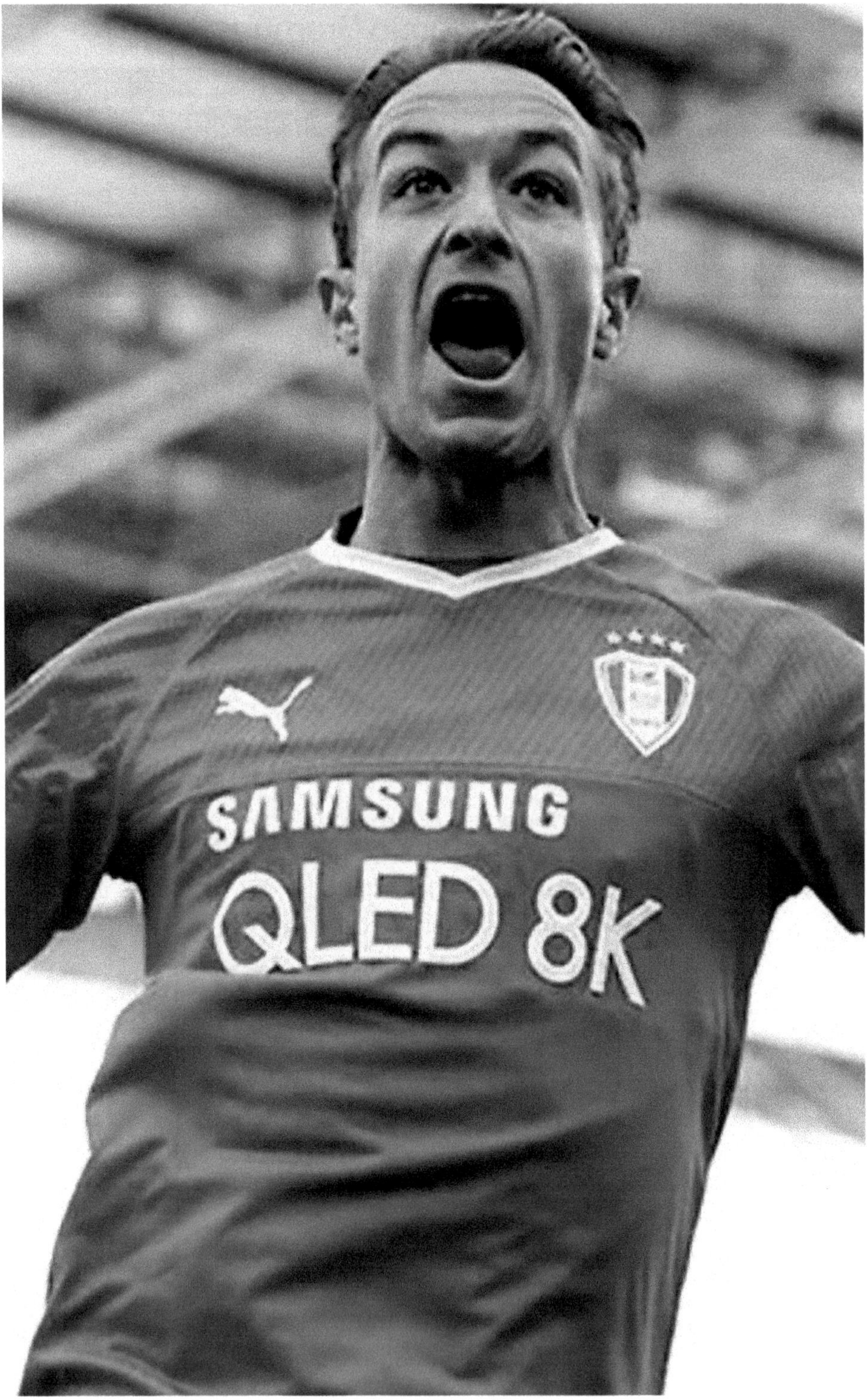
SAMSUNG
QLED 8K

Chapter 9
Adam Taggart
Suwon Samsung Bluewings, South Korea, 2019
(20 goals)

Adam Taggart is a Perth boy through and through, growing up out west he would go to Glory games when not playing his junior football with ECU Joondalup.

Taggart would eventually join the Glory and after a brief stint at the Australian Institute of Sport would go on to represent his home club in 10 games before crossing the country to join Newcastle United Jets in 2012.

It was here that his career would really flourish, playing alongside former Premier League players Emile Heskey and Michael Bridges, as well as 2008 A-League Golden Boot winner, Joel Griffiths. In season 2013/14, the young Taggart would top the chart with 16 goals in 25 games at the ripe old age of 21.

'It was a good time to be part of that team, probably one of my most enjoyable years in football. To play with those players was great. Training and playing with Premier League players tends to bring the best out of most people, it definitely does me, I like being around people who you can try and lift your standards.'

Heskey was 36 years old at the time and proved to be the perfect foil, scoring only once himself but taking the attention of the defenders:

'Heskey was known as someone who can support a goal scorer in all of the teams he has played in. He even stuck to that role at Newcastle, he didn't score a ton of goals but for me he was fantastic.

'[He was] One of my favourite people to play up front with, he is just so big and strong. A selfless striker, all those things mixed together added to a very enjoyable and successful year.'

Taggart's breakout A-League season earned him a spot in the Socceroos' squad for the 2014 World Cup in Brazil, where he featured in the group games against the Netherlands and Spain. It also secured him a contract in the United Kingdom where he signed with London club, Fulham.

His stint in the UK was anything but successful. The cycle of injury, surgery, recovery and re-injury saw him play a total of seven games in two seasons, and that was on loan with Dundee United in Scotland…and they ended up relegated!

'Playing catchup on those injuries took their toll. I don't think I played any football at all until the last four weeks of the first season I was there.

'The second season was similar. I started off in pre-season doing alright, then [I got] a small injury that took a lot longer for me to push back into training, and by the time I got fit, I was straight back out on loan to Scotland with a team fighting relegation.

'During my time in Scotland, I started to look at the next place I could go, I was at that stage that I just needed to play.'

It was back home at Perth Glory where Taggart could restart his football journey, and after a couple of seasons at home, the chance to work with legendary Australian striker and coach John Aloisi meant that Taggart signed with the Brisbane Roar.

However, the partnership in Queensland was short-lived as Aloisi was moved on. Taggart got itchy feet again about a move overseas, wanting his next move to be more successful than his UK stay.

In 2019, Suwon Bluewings in the Korea's K League came calling and soon enough Taggart had signed a one-year contract with an option for a further two years.

'They were looking for a striker and I was looking to explore my options overseas again and have a crack. It was an opportunity to go there with an open mind and Asia seemed to be a destination I started to look at a little closer as I was getting older.'

Similar to Japan, Korea has the 3 + 1 rule, where each side is allowed three foreigners and one foreigner from within the Asian confederation. Of the four foreigners that

Suwon had on their books for that season, three of them were strikers. Brazilian Wagner da Silva Souza (known as Waguininho) was one, and the other was Bosnian legend Dejan Damjanović. Although Damjanović was 37 years old in 2019, he had three K League Golden Boots in his kit bag.

'It was Damjanović or me nearly every time. If someone didn't have a great first half, we swapped. It was very rare that we got to play together.'

If Taggart was feeling the pressure as a foreign striker, he certainly didn't show it, scoring on debut 18 minutes after coming off the bench. Then in his first start, he managed two goals in a 3–1 victory.

The K League also had rules where they needed to start an Under-21 Korean player in all games, which made for some crazy substitutions, sometimes as early as the 20th minute mark.

'They make those selections just to tick that box and to get whoever they want on. I did that in my second game [came on in the 26th minute], I couldn't believe it. But that happens in every game across the League.'

Given the different culture, Korean coach and craziness of the substitutions, the role of the club interpreter became vitally important. Taggart was lucky enough to form a bond with club interpreter Johnny, who would become his friend.

'He could speak Portuguese, English and Korean. English was his third language. We became really good mates, he was a good guy and played a big part in my success at Suwon. We would go to dinner or a coffee, he is pretty much with you 24/7 around the club, he's on the away trips, game days, in the dressing room he's sitting right next to you. He's your 'go to' man for everything, which makes it quite easy as you only talk to the interpreter for anything.'

The bond between foreign player and interpreter needs to be strong so the interpreter can be selective in what messages are shared between player and manager.

'There were a lot of funny moments, the translator has to cop a lot of shit. Clearly being taken off at halftime, he cops a lot but can't translate it all to the manager, and sometimes if we're not happy with being taken off and we say something, he's not going to translate it back to the coach in Korean!'

Another relationship that Taggart developed was with teammate Yeom Ki-hun, the veteran winger who was a dead-ball specialist and known as the "assist man". He had played for the national team and holds the record for the most assists in the K League.

'He was a great player; he was quite old and had been at Suwon his whole career. He struggled with English but would speak to me through the interpreter a fair bit, a really good guy, super switched-on football wise.

'His left foot was a joke, not just set pieces but he set me up in a lot of games. A class player, I like having those people around at training also, it helps to lift the standard.'

Their relationship developed so much that later in the season he called a team meeting to tell his teammates that he would be handing over penalty-kicking duty to Taggart.

'In the meeting he told everyone that he was going to give the penalties to me now to help me get the Golden Boot.

'It helped me because I won by one goal and in the last couple of games, I did score some penalties.'

Taggart did indeed need those last two penalties as he finished the season on 20 goals, one ahead of Brazilian Junior Negrão from Ulsan Hyundai. This included four goals scored in the final five games of the season when the Korean League is divided into two groups of six to determine final places.

He revelled in the added pressure of being one of the foreign players in Korea.

'I really enjoyed that first year. It reignited my passion for the game, and I knew what I wanted to achieve in football at Suwon, the kind of footballer I wanted to be. It helped me enjoy football, stay motivated and absorb the pressure.

'The League has different levels of pressure to Australia; there's the threat of relegation, [and] big bonuses if you succeed. In general, there is a lot of pressure anyway and being a foreigner, you are made to feel the pressure from the start.'

Like the Aussies in Belgium a few decades earlier, Korea had a sub-culture of Australians looking after each other and Taggart's friendship with fellow Australian footballer Connor Chapman (who had played with four different Korean clubs) helped him settle into the country.

'Going there, I didn't know much about Korea. Connor was the guy I went to in order to find out a little bit about the culture. It's all about respect and age.

'That little bit of guidance from a mate who had been there helped me a lot. If you didn't have that you would be in for a big, big shock. It all adds to make it fresh and different. If you embrace it, it's really cool and there is so much history behind the place.'

The other plus for Taggart was the treatment of the foreigners. Being set up in luxury helps with your preparation.

'They really look after you and invest in you. They set me up with a four-bedroom, two-bathroom apartment. It was way too big for me; I didn't even go down one side of the place!'

Such was Taggart's success at Suwon that he even made a K League All-Stars line-up that took on Italian powerhouse Juventus at a packed-out Seoul Stadium. Taggart didn't realise how much he would enjoy the exhibition game but is glad he played.

'There are a lot of games to play in Korea with the League and Cup and friendlies, and when we were going into this Juventus game, I was almost dying for a rest.

'But being a part of it was just so much fun. I couldn't believe we were playing in front of a packed stadium in Seoul.'

Coming on after halftime, Taggart continued his goal-scoring form, netting against the Italians in the 50th minute as they played out a 3–3 draw.

'Playing just 45 minutes was so enjoyable. When the whistle went you were wanting it to go for a little longer as it was just loads of fun and you were like a kid playing in the schoolground again.'

Adam Taggart had an outstanding debut season at Suwon—Golden Boot, Player of the Month in July, Player of the Round twice and K League Team of the Year. They finished fourth but managed to win the Cup, which was the first team trophy that Taggart had ever won.

During 2020, the K League was one of the first leagues to start back after the COVID pandemic lockdowns. All world soccer eyeballs seemed to be on Korea with television coverage extending to Australia and gambling companies jumping on board the K League. It was one of the first competitions to play games in front of no crowds. That was something that Taggart took a while to get used to.

'It was a crazy first few months, being in another country and not being able to ply my trade. We knew that there would be a lot of people watching (on TV). But when you are at the stadium and there is no crowd there, it was a real weird feeling with no atmosphere, and you felt like you were playing a training game.

'A very strange feeling and that continued for all that season. I know that one of the reasons I like playing football is in front of people and playing in an empty stadium, it is almost awkward, you feel [like] you are running around naked.'

Infamously that season, FC Seoul had a solution for the lack of crowds—utilising blow up dolls to help fill the stands, although Taggart's Suwon Bluewings didn't feature in any of those bizarre matches.

COVID momentum and a new coach halted Taggart's second season in the K League (22 games for 8 goals), but his form was enough to earn him the move to the stronger Japanese League, with J1 League club Cerezo Ozaka signing him.

Taggart has now come full circle in his professional career. During the 2022/23 season, he signed again for Perth Glory, scoring two late goals off the bench in his first game back in an amazing welcome home with a 3–1 win over Melbourne Victory. Hopefully there is more of that to come for Adam Taggart.

Adam Taggart | Suwon Blue Wings | 2019

Round	H or A	Opposition	Score	Result	Goals
1	A	Ulsan Hyundai	2-1	L	1
2	H	Jeobuk Hyundai	0-4	L	0
3	A	Seongnam FC	2-1	L	0
4	H	Incheon Utd	3-1	W	2
5	H	Sangiu Sangmu	0-0	D	0
6	A	Gangwon FC	0-2	W	1
7	H	Daegu FC	0-0	D	0
8	A	Gyeongnam FC	3-3	D	1
9	A	Pohang Steelers	1-0	L	0
10	H	FC Seoul	1-1	D	0
11	A	Jeju United	1-3	W	1
12	H	Ulsan Hyundai	1-3	L	Did Not Play
13	A	Daegu FC	0-0	D	Did Not Play
14	H	Pohang Steelers	3-0	W	Did Not Play
15	H	Gangwon FC	1-1	D	0
16	A	FC Seoul	4-2	L	1
17	A	Jeonbuk Hyundai	1-1	D	1
18	H	Gyeongnam FC	0-0	D	0
19	H	Jeju United	2-0	W	1
20	A	Incheon Utd	2-3	W	2
21	A	Sangiu Sangmu	0-2	W	1
22	H	Seongnam FC	1-2	L	1
23	A	Daegu FC	0-2	W	1
24	H	Pohang Steelers	0-2	L	0
25	H	Incheon Utd	0-1	L	0
26	A	Gangwon FC	1-3	W	3
27	A	Gyeongnam FC	2-0	L	0
28	H	Jeju United	1-0	W	Did Not Play
29	A	Seongnam FC	0-0	D	0
30	H	Sangiu Sangmu	1-1	D	0
31	H	Ulsan Hyundai	0-2	L	0
32	A	Jeonbuk Hyundai	2-0	L	Did Not Play
33	H	FC Seoul	1-2	L	0
Group B1	H	Gyeongnam FC	2-1	W	1
Group B2	A	Incheon	1-1	D	1
Group B3	H	Seongnam FC	0-0	D	0
Group B4	A	Jeju United	2-4	W	2
Group B5	A	Sanju Sangmu	4-1	L	0

Chapter 10
Joey Gibbs
Keflavík, Iceland, 2020 (21 goals)

Joey Gibbs made his professional debut in 2010 in Australian football for Sydney FC in remarkable circumstances.

He came on as a substitute in extra time of that year's A-League Grand Final against Melbourne Victory in front of 44,000 fans at the Docklands Stadium. Replacing the injured Alex Brosque in the 115th minute, Gibbs' first taste of professional football resulted in a premiership win, a medal and a night of celebrations with the famed A-League trophy, known affectionately as the 'the toilet seat'.

An unsuccessful stint in Belgium with Olympic Charleroi netted zero senior games, so Gibbs came back to Australia to play in the New South Wales National Premier League (NPL) competition with Manly United. From there, he moved to former National Soccer League side, Marconi Stallions. At Marconi he won the NSW NPL Grand Final, and with 12 goals, made the NPL team of the season. This led to Gibbs joining the new A-League team Western Sydney Wanderers for their inaugural season in 2012/13.

He made his Wanderers debut in Round 4 of that season against Brisbane Roar—another memorable occasion as it was the first ever victory for Western Sydney, further cementing Gibbs' career in Australian football history.

However, he was released after one season with Western Sydney Wanderers after scoring twice in 13 games. A short trip north for the next A-League season saw Gibbs join Newcastle United Jets. In his third club debut in the A-League, he came off the bench against Brisbane Roar and scored with his first touch of the football.

Three quite remarkable debut games for three different A-League clubs.

But with the Jets' side boasting former Premier League goal scorers Emile Heskey and Michael Bridges, as well as young Australian Under-20 striker Adam Taggart, Gibbs found it hard to get a look in and only played four times that season.

So here you have the conundrum for an Australian striker—one good enough to get in the squad for three A-League clubs, but not quite there week-in, week-out to play regularly. He was a quality player in New South Wales at NPL level, but where could he take his career?

After Newcastle Jets, Gibbs joined APIA Leichhardt, another ex-NSL club in Sydney. Then he tried a brief stint playing in Hong Kong before returning to the NSW NPL and playing over 100 games with Blacktown City.

Gibbs summed up the struggle:

'I tend to reflect on it, when you are coming through as a young Australian striker, there are limited spots in the A-League to try and cement your spot. It's usually the position that a team will get a foreigner in to play. I am not complaining about it, that's the way it is, it's just difficult. Without a professional second division, it's the A-League or the NPL. The NPL is part-time, three days a week, you play in winter, [a] completely different time to the A-League. It's a tough circumstance compared to other places in the world.'

In 2020, the opportunity came to leave the NPL and play professionally overseas in Iceland—Gibbs jumped at the chance. So how does a player get to Iceland?

'It all happened very quickly. The club got in touch with my agent, and there was a few mutual connections. The club knew me as a footballer, [and] knew my coach who knew the Icelandic coach.

'It came about very quickly. After one week of chatting, the contract was there and I was in Iceland.'

Iceland is well-regarded as a country that punches well above its weight in world football. Never more so than in the 2016 Euros when they defeated England 2–1 in the Round of 16 and made the competition's Quarter-Finals. That tournament with the fans and their Viking Clap made the rest of the world sit up and take notice—a country with a population of around 325,000 people showed that it is able to compete on the world stage. The reason for their success is the country's devotion to the game at every level.

Gibbs joined Second Division club Knattspyrnudeild Keflavíkur, more commonly known as Keflavík. Based in the town of Reykjanesbær on the southern peninsula of Iceland, it is home to the Viking World Museum as well as the Iceland Museum of Rock 'n' Roll.

Here's an indication of how football-crazy Iceland is: the small population supports two divisions of professional teams, and the population of Reykjanesbær is just under 20,000 residents but has a 5,200-capacity stadium for Keflavík to play its home matches.

All coaches at every level in Iceland are UEFA-credited with a minimum of a B licence for juniors. They have indoor pitches and artificial turf so when the weather turns and the professional game goes into a seven-month recess, they can continue to practise and train. Gibbs walked straight into an amazing football culture.

'I didn't know too much about Iceland to be honest, but I did know, and it was confirmed to me when I was over there, that they do things quite well in football for such a small population. A great coach-education process and they do the right things and get the best out of the players they have.

'It's true there is such a passion for football, every young kid gets an opportunity to play and develop. All the coaches come across as very intelligent people.'

When it came to the professionalism of the Leagues in Iceland, there were no limitations on foreigners, visa spots or squad numbers due to the need for so many footballers in such a small place.

'There was a team in our League which had 12 [foreigners]. These small towns all have football teams, and some of the local Icelandic players aren't up to it, so they have to bring in foreigners to field a team.'

The chance for Gibbs to make himself a crowd favourite quickly evaporated as the COVID pandemic meant that initially only crowds of 500 were allowed to watch before they were completely banned from attending.

However, the pandemic also reduced the crowds when it came to sightseeing and Gibbs made the most of his time there, taking in the natural beauty of the country.

'It is one of the most beautiful countries on Earth. The landscape is something else, volcanic and old lava rock features and amazing hot springs and geysers with steam coming out of the ground. It's a phenomenal country. Even Reykjavik, the capital, is just a nice little cosy town, it's such a beautiful place. Everyone should visit Iceland if they can.

'Travelling around to see the natural beauty and tourist spots it was probably a great year to do it, because usually it's full of tourists but this year [2020], it wasn't. Me and some of the boys would just go for a drive around and see some amazing places.'

Gibbs had an amazing first season in Iceland, scoring on debut in a 5–1 win and never going more than one game without scoring. In that first season, he scored 21 goals from 19 games, including one hattrick and seven doubles.

'Everything went well for me from the start, I didn't get a chance to feel much pressure in a negative way. As a foreign striker, if you don't score goals you will get criticised, simple as that. I continued to score which meant I was getting praise from the media which is good.

'They just kept going in, the way the team played was very conducive to the way I score goals. You know crosses into areas where I make my runs and good delivery, good timing, and it worked well to the way I play.'

There were three waves of COVID-19 in Iceland. The third one brought the season to a premature end, but it was enough to award Keflavík the title, promotion to the First Division, and Gibbs the Golden Boot.

'It was a funny atmosphere at times. It was a weird season. On a personal level and on a team level, so much went well. Even when it came to winning the championship, we found that out after a four-week break because they suspended the season and then had to call it off.

'So we found out via a Facebook post and then had one night to celebrate before strict lockdown measures were coming into place. We were only allowed 20 people in a room to celebrate [with the restrictions]. It was obviously a great season, but very different.'

Since making it back to Iceland's top division, Keflavík have managed to stay there, narrowly avoiding relegation in 2021 after finishing 10th out of the 12 teams. Gibbs continued his goal-scoring form, finishing equal fourth in the Golden Boot with 10 goals (the winner scored 16) and in 2022 the team finished seventh. Gibbs found it tough with only three goals that season.

He turned 30 ahead of the 2023 season and is hoping to build on his achievements, transferring to fellow First Division Club, Stjarnan Gardabaer.

'From 28–32, you are in the prime of your career, so I am looking forward to playing my best football in Iceland for a few more seasons.'

Joey Gibbs | Keflavik | 2020

Round	H or A	Opposition	Score	Result	Goals
1	H	Afturelding	5-1	W	1
2	A	Víkingur	0-4	W	1
3	H	Leiknir	1-2	L	0
4	A	Grindavík	4-4	D	2
5	H	Thór	2-1	W	0
6	A	Thróttur	0-4	W	2
7	A	Leiknir	1-1	D	0
8	H	Vestri	4-1	W	2
9	A	ÍBV	1-3	W	2
10	H	Fram Reykjavík	1-1	D	0
11	A	Magni	1-4	W	3
12	H	Víkingur	6-1	W	2
13	A	Afturelding	2-2	D	1
14	A	Leiknir	5-1	L	0
15	No Game				
16	A	Thór	1-3	W	2
17	H	Thróttur	4-2	W	2
18	A	Vestri	1-3	W	1
19	H	ÍBV	3-1	W	0
20	H	Leiknir	2-1	W	0

Chapter 11
Nikita Rukavytsya
Maccabi Haifa, Israel, 2019/20
(18 goals)
Maccabi Haifa, Israel, 2020/21
(17 goals)

Nikita Vadymovych Rukavytsya was born in the Ukraine in 1987. He moved to Perth, Western Australia with his family at the age of 14. Rukavytsya first played junior football at Inglewood United, a club founded in 1951 by Ukrainian migrants and formerly known as Inglewood Kiev. From there he joined Perth SC, the biggest NPL club in Western Australia.

He was soon recognised as a prodigious talent with pace to burn and a rocket left boot. Within four years of his arrival 'Down Under', he was offered a football scholarship to the Australian Institute of Sport in Canberra.

In 2006, Perth Glory had appointed Ron Smith as their head coach. Smith had previously worked in development at the AIS and in his second season he decided to invest in young Western Australian talent. He immediately signed Rukavytsya.

'I tried to change the profile of the team and bring West Aussie players in around the Olympic age. That backfired on me as they kept disappearing on me for two weeks at a time for training camps.'

Despite his strong goal-scoring form in Perth's NPL, Rukavytsya couldn't find the back of the net for Smith or Perth Glory. Smith kept playing him and Perth Glory kept coming up short. According to Smith, it was all between the ears for his young marksman:

'With Nikita, I could feel the tension mounting because he hadn't scored. No matter what you say, it is a mental barrier. In the State League he was scoring goals for fun but in the A-League, Nikita couldn't shoot a fish in a barrel.'

After eleven rounds without a win, Glory management decided it was enough and sacked Smith from his role, and you wouldn't believe it, in the very next game Rukavytsya scored a brace as Glory got their first win of the season, 4–1 away at Newcastle under new coach David Mitchell. Two games later, it was another brace for Rukavytsya, at home against Melbourne Victory. Six goals in the final eight games of the season set him on his way according to Smith.

'It opened the floodgates on his career from then on. He scored on a regular basis and became really composed in front of goal.'

In 2009, the Professional Footballers Association of Australia awarded Rukavytsya the Harry Kewell Medal for the best Under-23 player.

After his domestic form, it became a matter of *where* he would end up playing overseas rather than *if*, and in a whirlwind six-year period he would play at the 2008 Beijing Olympics for the Olyroos, in Holland with FC Twente, in Belgium with KSV Roeselare, feature off the bench for the Socceroos in two of their group games at the 2010 World Cup in South Africa, and then play at German clubs Hertha BSC, Mainz 05 and FSV Frankfurt.

Looking for some stability, Rukavytsya re-joined the A-League in 2014/15 to play with Western Sydney Wanderers. It was the Wanderers' third season and after first and second finishes in their first two seasons, 2014/15 was completely underwhelming. They finished second last and managed only four wins.

Rukavytsya's glamorous model wife Vika is Israeli, so following the Wanderers' messy season he returned to European football, signing a one-year deal with Beita Jerusalem in the Israeli Premier League (IPL). It also allowed them to be closer to her family.

In Rukavytsya's first season in the IPL he was played on the wing. Using his pace, he managed to score 11 goals in 21 games, taking Beita Jerusalem to third place.

The rules in Israeli football are that you can have six foreign players in your squad, but only five of them can be on the pitch at the same time.

However, after Rukavytsya's first season in Israel, he was considered a local player due to his marriage to an Israeli. The two biggest Israeli clubs are Maccabi Haifi and

Maccabi Tel Aviv. Both of those clubs wanted to sign him after his first Israeli season, and Maccabi Haifa swooped and signed him on a three-year deal.

According to Israeli football journalist Ori Cooper, when Rukavytsya joined Haifa they were in a bit of a rut.

'When he arrived, he came at a really bad time. They had a lost decade; ten years where the team performed poorly. No matter how many players the coach bought, the team played poorly.'

Rukavytsya also suffered a little from expectations and the second-year blues, managing only two goals (both penalties) from 18 games as the team finished sixth. His second and third season returns at Haifa were a little better with seven goals in each, playing from the wing. The improvement of Haifa was evident with a second-placed season in 2018/19.

Cooper said that there was plenty of debate amongst the fans and the media about the best position to play Rukavytsya—

'There was a big debate in Israel if he should play on the wing, or as a striker or not at all in our League.'

Things changed for Nikita in the 2019/20 season when he was moved to play as the main striker for Haifa. With fellow Socceroo, defender Trent Sainsbury also at Haifa that season, Rukavytsya blitzed scoring 18 goals to win the Golden Boot comfortably. Home crowds were up as Haifa slogged it out with Maccabi Tel Aviv for the title, eventually falling short by six points.

Speaking on a podcast, Trent Sainsbury explained what it was like to play and live with Rukavytsya in Israel at that time:

'He is the king of Israel! King Niki! Any chance in front of goal, he would just put it on target. He is a deadly finisher and super quick for his age, he is rapid fast. It was a pleasure to play with him, and that Aussie connection helped me settle in a lot quicker. He was one of the good guys to hang off.'

Sainsbury also talked about the atmosphere when Rukavytsya was scoring in front of the home fans.

'They were the best fans I ever played in front of. They were crazy and you could feel the energy and the electricity in the air when we scored. It was a pleasure to play good football for them.'

Ori Cooper recalled that Haifa wanted to build on that season. In 2020/21, they went one step further and won the championship in a watershed year for the team.

'For season 2020/21, Haifa signed coach Barak Bakhar who is the best Israeli coach ever, and he took them to a new high.

'Nikita played magnificently, they won the championship, he was the top goal scorer, and it was a real achievement.'

Playing against the likes of Tottenham Hotspur in the Champions League that season, Rukavytsya was in such red-hot form that he broke the Haifa record for scoring in the most consecutive matches—12!

If you include him scoring in the Champions League, his 13 in a row was the longest run of consecutive goal-scoring games by any player in the world that season.

All of this was topped off in the final game of the season as Maccabi Haifa were crowned the champions of 2020/21 with a 3–2 win over Hapoel Be'er Sheva to stave off Maccabi Tel Aviv by one point. Rukavytsya scored the second goal of the match and his 17th in the League for the season, sealing the win and his second successive Golden Boot trophy.

It was a six-year lead-up to Rukavytsya being crowned Champion of Israel in a season that had to be stopped twice due to the pandemic. It was a just reward for a lot of hard work.

However, it was quickly back down to earth after that season for Rukavytsya. Haifa decided not to renew his contract and go in a different direction with younger strikers instead. He remained in Israel though, signing with Hapoel Be'er Sheva. Ori Cooper said:

'Haifa wanted to start a new era. Sheva are the third biggest club in Israel and they took him. When he signed, we weren't sure what he would give them. We weren't sure if he would be a starting XI player, but he did quite okay, scoring ten goals and helping Sheva finish second.'

Sheva finished second to his old club Maccabi Haifa, who managed to secure back-to-back championships. With Champions League football and plenty of games ahead of them, after one season away, Haifa re-signed Rukavytsya.

According to Ori Cooper, he doesn't quite have the pace that he used to, but he can still perform a role and that's why they re-signed him.

'Haifa decided to take him back, but this time as their third-string striker as they are playing a lot of matches. They needed a reliable third striker.'

At 35 years of age, it would appear to be the perfect role to finish an amazing career. Nikita Rukavytsya has scored the most goals by a foreigner in the history of the Israeli Premier League.

Nikita Rukavytsya | Maccabi Haifa | 2019/20

Round	H or A	Opposition	Score	Result	Goals
1	H	Hapoel Raanana	4-3	W	2
2	A	Hapoel Haifa	0-0	D	0
3	H	Kiryat Shmona	2-0	W	1
4	A	Maccabi Tel Aviv	1-0	L	0
5	H	Maccabi Netanya	3-0	W	1
6	A	Ness Ziona	0-3	W	1
7	H	Bnei Yehuda	1-1	D	0
8	A	Kfar Saba	0-3	W	0
9	A	Hapoel Tel Aviv	1-2	W	0
10	H	Beita Jerusalem	3-1	W	1
11	A	Hapoel Hadera	0-3	W	1
12	H	FC Ashdod	3-3	D	0
13	A	H.Beer Sheva	0-2	W	0
14	A	Hapoel Raanana	0-0	D	0
15	H	Hapoel Haifa	3-0	W	2
16	A	Kiryat Shmona	1-2	W	1
17	H	Maccabi Tel Aviv	3-4	L	1
18	A	Maccabi Netanya	0-2	W	1
19	H	Ness Ziona	4-0	W	1
20	A	Bnei Yehuda	1-3	W	1
21	H	Kfar Saba	0-1	L	0
22	H	Hapoel Tel Aviv	5-0	W	1
23	A	Beita Jerusalem	2-0	L	0
24	H	Happoel Hadera	1-0	W	1
25	A	FC Ashdod	1-2	W	1
26	H	H. Beer Sheva	4-0	W	1

Nikita Rukavytsya | Maccabi Haifa | 2020/21

Round	H or A	Opposition	Score	Result	Goals
1	A	Hapoel Hadera	1-2	W	2
2	H	H.Beer Sheva	3-1	W	2
3	H	Maccabi Tel Aviv	2-2	D	1
4	H	FC Ashdod	2-1	W	1
5	A	Hapoel Haifa	2-1	L	1
6	A	Kfar Saba	3-2	L	1
7	H	Beita Jerusalem	2-0	W	1
8	A	Kiryat Shmona	0-3	W	1
9	A	Bnei Sakhnin	0-3	W	0
10	H	Hapoel Tel Aviv	1-0	W	1
11	A	M.Petah Tikva	1-2	W	1
12	H	Bnei Yehuda	3-0	W	Did Not Play
13	A	Maccabi Netanya	0-2	W	1
14	H	Hapoel Hadera	1-0	W	0
15	A	H.Beer Sheva	1-1	D	0
16	H	Bnei Sakhnin	3-0	W	1
17	A	Maccabi Tel Aviv	2-1	L	0
18	H	Kfar Saba	3-0	W	2
19	A	FC Ashdod	1-0	L	0
20	H	Hapoel Haifa	2-0	W	Did Not Play
21	A	Beita Jerusalem	0-3	W	Did Not Play
22	H	Kiryat Shmona	4-2	W	Did Not Play
23	A	Hapoel Tel Aviv	1-2	W	Did Not Play
24	H	M.Petah Tikva	0-2	L	Did Not Play
25	A	Bnei Yehuda	0-2	W	0
26	H	Maccabi Netanya	2-0	W	1

Chapter 12
Sam Kerr

Sky Blue FC, USA, 2017 (17 goals)
Chicago Red Stars, USA, 2018 (16 goals)
Chicago Red Stars, USA, 2019 (19 goals)
Chelsea, UK, 2020/21 (21 goals)
Chelsea, UK, 2021/22 (19 goals)

On the football pitch when it comes to scoring goals, Sam Kerr always appears to be in the right place at the right time. Her career has seemed to mirror this approach. The growth and professionalism of women's football has mirrored the rise and rise of Kerr.

She is without peer when it comes to Australian strikers–male or female–and their records overseas. If you include her two A-League Women's Golden Boot awards (13 goals in 2017/18 and 13 goals in 2018/19) when she was forced to play two seasons in a calendar year due to the semi-professional nature of women's football, she has won seven Golden Boot Awards in six years in three different Leagues on three different continents.

John Kosmina described her as the ultimate goal-scoring predator.

'A great finisher with a real instinct and eye for a goal. Unlike other strikers coming off the line, she has a real sense of where the goals are and when to score. She's just a natural goal scorer.'

For the first time in 2018/19, the Women's Super League in England's Football Association became fully professional and Kerr was lured away from the USA to high-profile London club, Chelsea. Under the leadership of Emma Hayes, Kerr has won trophy after trophy and scored goal after goal ever since.

The rise in professionalism has also seen Kerr benefit financially. Sponsored by Nike, she features heavily in their marketing via their advertising campaigns and on billboards. In 2023, for the first time ever, the EA video game FIFA featured women's club teams and they put Sam Kerr in her Chelsea kit on the cover, along with French and Paris Saint-Germain male superstar Kylian Mbappé.

Over 325 million copies of this game have been sold worldwide. It is a big deal and Kerr is a big deal.

A billboard of her backflipping celebration in her Chelsea kit adorns the outside of Stamford Bridge. Her children's book series *Kicking Goals* is close to becoming a best-seller for young girls and boys in Australia.

Her marketability is also without peer and as the Australian captain of the Matildas, she appeals to children and sports' fans Down Under of both genders. Initially, it was her signature back-flip goal celebrations which made her standout, but it has become more than that with her consistent performances on the pitch. As the leading goal scorer of Super League powerhouse Chelsea, she is recognisable as one of the best players in the world plying her trade in Europe, and her Kolkata heritage via her Indian paternal grandmother means she is also making inroads with the South Asian community.

Kerr's sporting genes run deep. There is no denying that her talent is in her blood— if you look at her family, you can see sporting prowess everywhere. Her paternal grandparents were enthusiastic amateur sportspeople in India. Her father Roger had a successful career playing and coaching Australian Rules football. Her mother Roxanne had uncles and fathers who played Australian Rules in the Western Australian state Leagues and Kerr's older brother Daniel played more than 200 games with the West Coast Eagles, winning a premiership and gaining All-Australian honours. She is even related to a Melbourne Cup-winning jockey in J.J. Miller, who is her mother's uncle. He won the famous horse race in 1966 aboard Galilee.

With so much Australian Rules football in her family and Western Australia being a crazy Australian Rules state, it is no surprise to learn that 'footy' was originally Sam Kerr's game. She played as a junior until age 12, and when she was no longer able to play with the boys, she reluctantly moved to play the beautiful game.

Playing football in the middle-class Perth suburb of Mosman Park started for Kerr at the Western Knights. Amazingly, within three years of starting, she would be a senior Matilda.

Kerr made her Australian debut against Italy in Canberra in 2009 as a 15-year-old under coach Tom Sermanni. Her rapid rise meant that by age 18 she had played three seasons for Perth Glory in the W-League (now the A-League Women) as well as 18 senior games for the Matildas, including the 2010 Asian Cup victory. She scored the Matilda's only goal in open play in the Asian Cup Final, as well as the first penalty in the shoot-out win over North Korea.

In 2013 when the National Women's Soccer League (NWSL) started in the USA, Kerr moved abroad and joined the Western New York Flash. At only 20 years of age, it was a big move for Kerr and it would begin a period of seven years where she would play in the northern summer in the USA, followed by the Australian summer in the W-League. She played for Perth Glory and Sydney FC in Australia and Western New York Flash, Sky Blue FC (New Jersey) and the Chicago Red Stars in the USA.

It was during this period of non-stop football that Kerr suffered a Lisfranc injury, sustained whilst playing at Perth Glory. It was the second major injury of her career and put her in doubt for the 2016 Rio Olympics. According to her Sky Blue FC coach, she worked so hard to make the Olympics with both their medical team and the Matildas' medical team working hard to help her:

'The amount of work that Kerr did around Rio to get herself fit was incredible. She got back into great condition. The Aussies didn't want her to play before the Olympics, but we had to beg, borrow and steal to allow her to play before Rio.

'The first game back from injury she scored an absolutely cracking goal against Washington Spirit. It was nice for Sam and it was so much relief. It was reward for her hard work and she could go off to the Olympics.'

At the Olympics, the Matildas would reach the Round of 16 and lose out to the host nation Brazil on penalties. Kerr managed one goal in the Group stages against Germany. It proved to be the launchpad for Kerr to take her career to the next level and her time in the States after the Olympics would be the making of her as a footballer.

The light-bulb moment for Kerr came in a game against Kansas City. Trailing 2-0, she scored a 12-minute hattrick for Sky Blue to win the game. Her coach remembered it:

'If you look at Sam's involvement in all three of those goals, [it was] absolutely world class, from the movement to the combinations to the finish. It was frightening some of the things she did in that game.'

Speaking with former Sky Blue FC teammate Kelley O'Hara as part of the *Just Women's Sports* podcast, Kerr succinctly remembered her thinking at the time:

'I realised I could play.'

Thriving on being the underdog at Sky Blue FC, Kerr scored and scored that season, and was involved in some crazy games as well.

She finished the season with 17 goals from 22 games and won the NWSL Golden Boot, as well as the League award for Most Valuable Player. She told O'Hara:

'That Sky Blue season was the first season I played as the 9. I found my position!'

In 2017, the Matildas competed at the Tournament of Nations in the USA. A four-country friendly tournament, Australia was up against the USA, Japan and Brazil. Kerr continued her form by scoring a hattrick against Japan—which resulted in more people paying attention to both her and the Matildas as Australia lifted the trophy.

Kerr found herself in a post-season, three-way trade that saw her join the Chicago Red Stars for season 2018.

Three-way trades are not common in the United States, but the Kerr trade was a little complex as it involved high-profile USA national team players Carli Lloyd (Houston to Sky Blue FC) and Christen Press (Chicago Red Stars to Houston) changing teams as well. Lloyd was a two-time FIFA World Player of the Year and Press a darling of the national team.

Australian women's football journalist, Samantha Lewis, spoke of the move:

'Her trade to Chicago was unusual, as she was traded with Nikki Stanton who was her teammate and her partner at the time.

'It is an indication of the stature that Sam Kerr had, when you have two sensational national team players of the USA who were part of the trade deal in Carli Lloyd and Christen Press.

'Moving to Chicago and a more professional setup than Sky Blue, she was now surrounded by higher-quality players. The more competitive environment at training would have helped as well.'

The Chicago coaching staff told me of the complexity of the trade deal.

'It took some patience. It took four to six weeks to finalise and then it was on or off six or seven times leading up to the draft and literally the night before the draft, we had agreed on all the terms, but then the day of the draft things had changed. We were very fortunate that the deal got done.'

The trade paid off for Kerr and Chicago Red Stars—Kerr's 2018 season saw her win her second Golden Boot in a row, scoring 16.

Chicago's coach believed that the quality of her teammates would help her evolve.

'I think we got Sam around players who were putting balls into her, Julie Ertz and Alyssa Naeher, [they were] big personalities and big players who had won [the] World Cup, as well as her partnership with Japanese international Yuki Nagasato.

'I think she grew up when she was here too, because of being around those kinds of players and how they go about their business and what they did. We were super excited to have Sam.'

The 2019 NWSL season was interrupted by the Women's World Cup held in France. Kerr had developed so much as a player that she was made captain of the Matildas for the tournament. It was a surprise appointment to some in Australia, but not to her American coaches. According to her former Sky Blue coach:

'Sam is a very addictive person; she has the personality that you want to be around and she can galvanise the locker room.

'She is respected because she is hard working and always honest.

'At training she wants to do extra work and she asks questions in a respectful manner and on the pitch she will press until the 90th minute.'

Similar traits were seen when she was at the Chicago Red Stars according to her coaches.

'She is inclusive and generally cares about the whole group and not just herself.

'As much as she cares about scoring goals, she cares about winning more. If Sam scored five and the team lost 6–5, she wouldn't feel good about her five. That's a rare quality from a striker.

'She has positive energy and the thing for her to grow into becoming a captain is understanding when and where are the times to be serious and the times to joke around. From the moment she arrived at Chicago until the time she left, her biggest growth was understanding what the team needed at that moment.'

Australia progressed to the knockout stages of the 2019 World Cup, thanks largely to Kerr's four goals in a 4–1 trouncing of lowly-placed Jamaica. In the Round of 16 game against Norway, they lost on penalties, with Kerr missing the crucial first spot kick for the Aussies.

The Chicago Red Stars needed her back and refreshed, so she was offered some extra time to recover and get ready to finish the season. It was a tough decision for the coaches, as they hadn't scored a goal or won a game in her absence, and on the back of four consecutive losses they were facing an away trip to Orlando. Speaking to O'Hara again, Kerr summed up her thinking:

'After the World Cup, I was sitting on a beach in France having a break and I thought I need to play football.'

She met the team for that away game in Orlando and without training with her teammates, she started and finished the game, scoring a hattrick in a 3–2 win. Her Chicago coach was amazed.

'I wasn't expecting her for another ten days or so, but she wanted to get back with the group.

'She travelled with the team, she asked to start, 90 minutes later, three goals to Sam later, we win 3–2. Unbelievable. We were waiting for her to signal to come off, but she scored within the first five minutes. The whole confidence level and energy of the group just raised!'

Nineteen goals in season 2019 was enough for Kerr to win her third consecutive Golden Boot in the USA. That season, the Chicago Red Stars finished runners-up.

On the back of her incredible USA career, Kerr signed a two-and-a-half-year contract to join Chelsea in the English Football Association's Women's Super League (FAWSL), joining them for the end of the 2019/20 season. With women's football becoming increasingly more prominent, Kerr joined a large Australian contingent that moved to the UK to play with big clubs such as Arsenal, West Ham, Manchester City and Everton.

She started slowly at Chelsea with only one goal in her first seven games. However, her second season at the Blues in 2020/21 was her first full season and it saw her live up to the hype. Forming a deadly strike partnership with England international Fran Kirby and under the management of Emma Hayes, Kerr would take all before her in a season that saw Chelsea win the title, the FA Community Shield and the FA Women's League Cup. They also made the Final of the European Champions League, missing out 4–0 to Barcelona.

Kerr's work up front with Kirby, coined 'Kerr-by' by the media, saw her finish the season with 21 goals and seven assists, while Kirby had 16 goals and 11 assists.

Emma Hayes spoke about 'Kerr-by' after that first season together:

'If you had asked Sam if she could find anyone to service her with goals like Yuki Nagasato did [in the US with Chicago Red Stars] I think she would have questioned whether that would be the case. Sam was looking forward to playing with Fran Kirby more than any other player in our squad, because she saw the potential between them and vice versa. They just get each other.'

Kerr finished the season three goals ahead of Arsenal's Dutch superstar Vivianne Miedema and took that form into the Olympics, with goals against New Zealand and Sweden before scoring twice against Great Britain in an extra-time win to see the Matilda's progress to the Semi-Finals.

Following the Olympics, Kerr signed a contract extension for a further two years at the Blues and will be at Chelsea until the end of the 2023/24 season.

With international television coverage of the competition, more and more people have been able to appreciate what she is achieving on the pitch in the UK.

In 2021, Kerr made headlines back in Australia when she knocked a pitch invader to the ground with an Australian Rules style hip and shoulder during a Champions League tie against Juventus. Kerr's treatment of the fan drew praise from supporters— but the ire of the referee—receiving a yellow card for her physicality.

The 2021/22 season at Chelsea saw more honours and trophies come Kerr's way. The team won the League and the FA Cup, and Kerr's 19-goal season saw her win her second FAWSL Golden Boot in a row. This time she was five goals clear of Miedema.

Her form into the 2022/23 season with Chelsea and ahead of a home Women's World Cup with the Matildas continued. Kerr is entering the prime age bracket for elite strikers.

Former Socceroo striker Gary Cole is a Chelsea fan and can't stop admiring the work Kerr does playing football.

'She is just a joy to watch, seeing how quickly she has risen to the top and been able to stay there, she is just the complete player.

'Modern-day strikers spend more of their time facing forwards than they do facing backwards, as we used to do. She can still do that, play the ball off and make forward runs, she runs in behind really well and she always reminds me of Tim Cahill with her aerial ability. Just being able to read it and arrive at the right place at the right time with her head.

'She is technically very good using both feet and can bring people into the game as well, [she has] a great passing range and [is] just a fantastic all-round footballer.

'Strikers will have a couple of great seasons, but she just has the gift to not only finish well but be in the right place at the right time. You can give players hints and tips about that, but some strikers have just got the gift!'

In public, Kerr always pivots to the team and acknowledges that she is just one part of a bigger system. Coming from a time when the game was part-time to being a full-time professional playing in England, Kerr knows how hard female players had to work to get where they are now. Watch her at any Matildas or Chelsea game and she is always making time for the fans afterwards, especially the younger female fans, with autographs and selfies.

Her drive to succeed and get better is infectious, and admired universally by her coaches, teammates, opposition and fans.

Mark Schwarzer spoke to Kerr on Optus Sport about her 2021/22 season and how she was progressing as a footballer. She replied:

'Last year I won the Golden Boot, but I was prouder of all the big-moment goals I scored.

'As a striker it's what I pride myself on, being able to come up big when my team needs me.'

Kerr spoke to the BBC about the individual accolades that were coming her way and she summed up her team-first approach with this answer:

'The most important individual award for me is the Golden Boot. If I'm winning that, then the team is probably winning the title!'

Along with her five overseas Golden Boot titles, Kerr's individual accolades include the 2018 Young Australian of the Year, as well as being awarded the Order of Australia Medal in 2022.

There is no question that she will add to these over the coming football seasons and tournaments. Kerr is without question an outstanding athlete, an outstanding Australian captain and an outstanding role model.

Sam Kerr | Sky Blue FC | 2017

Round	H or A	Opposition	Score	Result	Goals
1	A	Seattle Reign	1-1	D	0
2	A	Boston Breakers	1-0	L	0
3	H	FC Kansas City	1-0	W	Did Not Play
4	A	Washington Spirit	4-3	L	0
5	A	Houston Dash	1-3	W	1
6	H	Houston Dash	2-1	W	0
7	A	North Carolina Courage	2-0	L	0
8	H	Orlando Pride	2-1	W	1
9	H	Portland Thorns	0-2	L	0
10	A	Portland Thorns	1-3	W	2
11	A	Chicago Red Stars	2-1	L	0
12	H	Orlando Pride	2-3	L	1
13	A	North Carolina Courage	0-1	W	1
14	H	FC Kansas City	3-2	W	3
15	H	Chicago Red Stars	2-2	D	1
16	A	Seattle Reign	5-4	L	1
17	H	Washington Spirit	1-4	L	Did Not Play
18	A	Orlando Pride	5-0	L	0
19	H	Seattle Reign	5-4	W	4
20	H	Boston Breakers	1-0	W	1
21	A	FC Kansas City	4-1	L	0
22	H	Washington Spirit	1-2	L	0
23	H	North Carolina Courage	1-1	D	0
24	A	Boston Breakers	3-4	W	1

Sam Kerr | Chicago Red Stars | 2018

Round	H or A	Opposition	Score	Result	Goals
1	A	Houston Dash	1-1	D	Did Not Play
2	H	Portland Thorns	2-3	L	Did Not Play
3	A	Utah Royals	0-1	W	Did Not Play
4	H	Houston Dash	3-0	W	Did Not Play
5	H	Sky Blue FC	1-1	D	Did Not Play
6	A	Washington Spirit	1-1	D	0
7	H	Orlando Pride	0-2	L	0
8	A	North Carolina Courage	1-1	D	1
9	H	Houston Dash	2-2	D	1
10	A	Seattle Reign	0-0	D	0
11	H	Orlando Pride	2-5	L	2
12	A	Washington Spirit	0-2	W	1
13	H	Portland Thorns	1-1	D	0
14	H	Utah Royals	2-0	W	0
15	H	Washington Spirit	2-0	W	0
16	A	North Carolina Courage	4-1	L	0
17	A	Sky Blue FC	1-3	W	3
18	H	Seattle Reign	1-0	W	1
19	H	North Carolina Courage	1-1	D	1
20	A	Seattle Reign	0-0	D	0
21	A	Portland Thorns	2-2	D	2
22	A	Orlando Pride	1-3	W	2
23	H	Sky Blue FC	5-0	W	1
24	A	Utah Royals	2-1	L	1
Semi-Final	A	North Carolina Courage	2-0	L	0

Sam Kerr | Chicago Red Stars | 2019

Round	H or A	Opposition	Score	Result	Goals
1	A	North Carolina Courage	1-1	D	1
2	H	Portland Thorns	4-4	D	1
3	H	Seattle Reign	3-0	W	0
4	A	Utah Royals	1-0	L	0
5	H	North Carolina Courage	3-1	W	2
6	A	Houston Dash	1-2	W	2
7	H	Washington Spirit	0-2	L	Did Not Play
8	A	Portland Thorns	3-0	L	Did Not Play
9	H	Seattle Reign	0-1	L	Did Not Play
10	A	Orlando Pride	2-3	W	3
11	H	Sky Blue FC	1-2	L	0
12	A	Houston Dash	0-1	W	0
13	H	North Carolina Courage	2-1	W	1
14	A	Seattle Reign	0-4	W	1
15	H	Utah Royals	2-0	W	1
16	A	Washington Spirit	1-0	L	0
17	A	Sky Blue FC	2-1	L	1
18	H	Orlando Pride	1-2	L	0
19	A	Portland Thorns	3-0	L	0
20	H	Houston Dash	3-0	W	2
21	A	Orlando Pride	0-1	W	0
22	A	Sky Blue FC	0-3	W	1
23	H	Washington Spirit	3-1	W	2
24	H	Utah Royals	2-1	W	1
Semi-Final	A	Portland Thorns	0-1	W	1
Final	A	North Carolina Courage	0-4	L	0

Sam Kerr | Chelsea | 2020/21

Round	H or A	Opposition	Score	Result	Goals
1	A	Manchester United	1-1	D	1
2	H	Bristol City	9-0	W	1
3	A	Birmingham City	0-1	W	0
4	H	Manchester City	3-1	W	1
5	H	Everton	4-0	W	1
6	A	Arsenal	1-1	D	0
7	H	West Ham	3-2	W	3
8	A	Brighton & Hove Albion	0-1	W	1
9	A	Reading	0-5	W	1
10	H	Manchester United	2-1	W	0
11	A	Aston Villa	0-4	W	0
12	H	Tottenham Hotspur	4-0	W	0
13	H	Brighton & Hove Albion	1-2	L	1
14	H	Arsenal	3-0	W	0
15	A	Bristol City	0-5	W	1
16	A	West Ham	0-2	W	1
17	A	Everton	0-3	W	0
18	H	Aston Villa	2-0	W	2
19	H	Birmingham City	6-0	W	3
20	A	Manchester City	2-2	D	1
21	A	Tottenham Hotspur	0-2	W	2
22	H	Reading	5-0	W	1

Sam Kerr | Chelsea | 2021/22

Round	H or A	Opposition	Score	Result	Goals
1	A	Arsenal	3-2	L	0
2	H	Everton	4-0	W	2
3	A	Manchester United	1-6	W	2
4	H	Brighton & Hove Albion	3-1	W	1
5	H	Leicester City	2-0	W	0
6	A	Aston Villa	0-1	W	0
7	A	Manchester City	0-4	W	1
8	H	Birmingham City	5-0	W	3
9	A	Reading	1-0	L	0
10	H	West Ham	2-0	W	0
11	H	Tottenham Hotspur	2-1	W	1
12	A	Everton	0-3	W	1
13	A	Brighton & Hove Albion	0-0	D	0
14	H	Manchester City	1-0	W	0
15	H	Arsenal	0-0	D	0
16	A	West Ham	1-4	W	1
17	H	Aston Villa	1-0	W	1
18	A	Leicester City	0-9	W	1
19	H	Reading	5-0	W	2
20	A	Tottenham Hotspur	1-3	W	1
21	A	Birmingham City	0-1	W	0
22	H	Manchester United	4-2	W	2

Chapter 13
Other Australian Goal-Scoring Feats

Richard Porta
2 Golden Boots
River Plate Montevideo, Uruguay, 2007/08 (19 goals)
River Plate Montevideo, Uruguay, 2011/12 (17 goals)

As featured in 'Surfing for England', Richard Porta was born in Sydney to Uruguayan parents, who all returned to live in Uruguay when Porta was quite young. Nicknamed 'El Canguro' (which is Spanish for 'kangaroo'), Porta featured three times for the Uruguayan Under-20 team. He was considered for Australian underage representative teams and the senior national team, however eligibility and communication problems meant he never played for Australia. He had a successful domestic career in Uruguay, winning two Golden Boots and he also played abroad in the Middle East.

Aleksandar Duric (Singapore)
4 Golden Boots

Singapore Armed Forces, 2007 (37 goals)
Singapore Armed Forces, 2008 (28 goals)
Singapore Armed Forces, 2009 (28 goals)
Tampines Rovers, Singapore, 2013 (25 goals)

Aleksander Duric's sporting career is quite extraordinary. Born in the former Yugoslavia, Duric represented Bosnia at the 1992 Barcelona Olympics in rowing. He later emigrated to Australia to try and embark on a football career. Given a lifeline by Frank Arok and Ange Postecoglou at South Melbourne, Duric had a nomadic Australian career in the NSL and NPL, playing for South Melbourne, Port Melbourne, Gippsland Falcons, West Adelaide, Heidelberg United, Marconi and Sydney Olympic.

While playing in the National Soccer League, he gained Australian citizenship and met his Australian wife, Natasha. His Gippsland Falcons' teammate and Australian legend Eddie Krncevic was the best man at their wedding.

When his Australian career finished, in another example of the kindness and support that Krncevic provided to fellow footballers, he helped secure Duric a move to Singapore, and he never looked back from there.

Duric won four domestic Golden Boot titles in the S-League, as well as representing the Singapore national team 53 times for 24 goals. His first game for Singapore came at age 37. He was the first foreign-born player to captain Singapore and at 42 years and 105 days he is the second-oldest player on record to have scored in international football.

Jason Cummings (Scotland)
2 Golden Boots
Hibernian, 2014/15 (18 goals)
Hibernian, 2016/17 (19 goals)

Jason Cummings was born in Scotland, but his grandparents were 'ten pound poms' who migrated to Australia in the 1960s and had two children before returning to Scotland.

Cummings won his first Golden Boot in the Scottish Championship for Hibernian in 2014/15 and then shared the award with Queen of the South's Stephen Dobbie in 2016/17 when Hibernian earned promotion back into the Scottish Premiership.

This form led to Cummings being capped for the Scotland National Team in 2017 in a friendly against the Netherlands.

Joining the Central Coast Mariners in 2022, he was able to switch allegiances to the Socceroos due to his mother being born in Perth, Western Australia.

Cummings scored on debut for the Socceroos against New Zealand and then represented his adopted country at the 2022 World Cup, playing in the group match against eventual winners Argentina.

The Socceroos and
Archie Thompson

Less than 3,000 people were at Coffs Harbour on 11 April 2001 to watch the Socceroos take on American Samoa in a World Cup Qualifier, but they saw both the Australian team and striker Archie Thompson break goal-scoring records.

Australia scored 31 goals to nil, with Thompson netting 13. These are still FIFA records for World Cup Qualifiers. American Samoa was horribly out of their depth, and it was a contributing factor in Australia lobbying to leave the weaker Oceania qualifying group for the stronger Asian federation not long afterwards.

FIFA underage tournaments

Some of Australia's male strikers have managed to top Golden Boot charts in FIFA underage tournaments:

1981 Under-20 World Championship
Mark Koussas (4 goals)

Held in Australia, Koussas finished equal first with Ralph Loose (Germany), Roland Wohlfarth (Germany) and Taher Abouzaid (Egypt).

1993 Under-20 World Championship
Ante Milicic (3 goals)

Also held in Australia, Milicic was the equal leading goal scorer with Gian (Brazil), Adriano (Brazil), Chris Faklaris (USA), Nieto (Mexico), Henry Zambrano (Colombia) and Augustine Ahinful (Ghana).

1995 Under-17 World Championship
Danny Allsop (5 goals)

Held in Ecuador, Allsop finished equal first with Mohammed Al-Kathiri (Oman).

Oceania Football Confederation Nations Cup

Australia has had the following Golden Boot winners:

1980 Ian Hunter and Eddie Krncevic (5 goals)
1996 Kris Trajanovski (7 goals)
1998 Damian Mori (10 goals)
2000 Craig Foster and Clayton Zane (5 goals)
2002 Joel Porter and Bobby Despotovski (5 goals, equal first with Chris Killen and Jeff Campbell from New Zealand)
2004 Tim Cahill (5 goals, equal first with Vaughan Coveny from New Zealand)

All-time Australian goal-scoring records as at 12 April 2023

Top Ten Goal Scorers

SOCCEROOS — all internationals

66 George Smith (1933–1939, 26 matches)

56 Gordon Nunn (1948–1958, 52 matches)

51 Tim Cahill (2004–2017, 109 matches)

49 Frank Parsons (1948–1951, 26 matches)

45 Alec Cameron (1927–1936, 46 matches)

42 John Kosmina (1976–1988, 100 matches)

35 Attila Abonyi (1967–1977, 89 matches)

34 Graham Arnold (1985–1997, 85 matches)

29 John Aloisi (1997–2007, 57 matches)

29 Damian Mori (1992–2002, 49 matches)

MATILDAS — all internationals

63 Sam Kerr (2009– , 120 matches)

47 Lisa De Vanna (2004–2019, 157 matches)

43 Kate Gill (2001–2015, 91 matches)

42 Cheryl Salisbury (1994–2009, 171 matches)

38 Sarah Walsh (2004–2012, 76 matches)

31 Linda Hughes (1989–2000, 78 matches)

30 Emily van Egmond (2010– , 128 matches)

29 Joanne Peters (1996–2009, 116 matches)

29 Kyah Simon (2007– , 112 matches)

29 Caitlin Foord (2011– , 109 matches)

AUS MEN'S NATIONAL LEAGUE

240 Damian Mori (1989–2007/08, 447 matches)

142 Besart Berisha (2011/12–2020/21, 236 matches)

140 Jamie Maclaren (2013/14– , 199 matches)

137 Rod Brown (1983–1997/98, 346 matches)

133 John Kosmina (1977–1989, 289 matches)

129 Archie Thompson (1996/97–2015/16, 334 matches)

127 Pablo Cardozo (1990/91–2003/04, 303 matches)

124 Francis Awaritefe (1989–2000/01, 323 matches)

123 Bobby Despotovski (1994/95–2006/07, 265 matches)

121 Marshall Soper (1981–1994/95, 318 matches)

AUS WOMEN'S NATIONAL LEAGUE

94 Michelle Heyman (2008/09– , 159 matches)

70 Sam Kerr (2008/09–2018/19, 95 matches)

67 Lisa De Vanna (2001/02–2021/22, 145 matches)

67 Kate Gill (1998/99–2014/15, 119 matches)

58 Tameka Yallop (2008/09–2020/21, 139 matches)

50 Kyah Simon (2008/09–2019/20, 108 matches)

46 Emily Gielnik (2010/11–2020/21, 109 matches)

46 Leena Khamis (2003/04–2021/22, 144 matches)

45 Tara Andrews (2009/10–2022/23, 131 matches)

44 Ashleigh Sykes (2008/09–2021/22, ~~105~~ matches)

Acknowlededgments

A book like this comes together thanks to the generosity of many football people - those who have given me their time through interviews, warm referrals, statistics, articles, book referrals, YouTube clips and anecdotes.

It was fantastic to sit down and talk all things Belgium, football and beer with Eddie Krncevic, Frank Farina and Aurelio Vidmar.

Joey Gibbs and Adam Taggart both gave me their time whilst in hotel isolation and were so generous with their stories.

Scott Ollerenshaw, Ron Smith and Declan Hill's discussions on Malaysian football and how it was run and won in the turbulent 1990s helped me to piece together Olly's time there.

Sam Lewis gave me her encyclopaedic knowledge of Sam Kerr and women's football. It's awesome to see Lewis' media profile rise in line with the rise of women's football.

As always, Andrew Howe, Gary Cole and John Kosmina (who are legends of the Australian game) were willing to assist me with stats, comments and opinions.

Scott McDonald's love and passion for Celtic was obvious in our chat and I hope I did his chapter justice.

Celtic Football Club and Glasgow City archivist Michael Gallagher had a wealth of material for me on Mark Viduka and Scott McDonald (and Michael even gave me his seat next to his Dad for a Celtic home game back in 2022, there is nothing like hugging strangers after a goal!).

Ori Cooper's knowledge and contribution to Israeli football helped me unravel Nikita Rukavytsya's quiet start in Israel to his two-season goal rush.

You would struggle to find a more passionate fan of Nagoya Grampus, Josh Kennedy and Japanese football than Kazane Kuwahara. I thank him for his detailed stories and Josh's song.

A special thanks to Lucas Gillard, Mark Boric, Garry McKenzie, Greg Stock, George Cotsanis, Greg Werner, Paul Mavroudis, Tony Persoglia, Ian Syson, Roy Hay,

Josh Parish, Lachie Flannigan and Neil Symons for all that they do for Australian football and Australian football history.

A big thanks to Chicago Red Stars, Joey Gibbs and Kazane Kuwhara for providing pictures.

To the Socceroos and Matildas who gave their time, there is nothing like tournament football to really reflect what you mean to me.

Finally, to Bonita Mersiades and Fair Play Publishing, you are an amazing vehicle to share our wonderful football stories. I could not be more grateful for the opportunities you afford me.

(Please note that I have deliberately not mentioned the name of some of the people I talked with in relation to Sam Kerr as they were subsequently banned from the NWSL in the USA, for matters unrelated to Kerr).

Bibliography and related sources

The following books, newspapers, magazines, websites and podcasts were used in the research for *Green and Golden Boots*.

Duric, Aleksandar & Wray, Glenn, *Beyond Borders,* Marshall Cavendish, 2016

Farina, Frank & Mersiades, Bonita, *My World is Round*, Vox Peritus, 1998

Goldsmith, Jason, *Surfing for England - Our lost Socceroos*, Fair Play Publishing, 2019

Hall, Matthew, *The Away Game*, Fair Play Publishing, 2020

Howe, Andrew & Werner, Greg, *Encyclopedia of Matildas*, Fair Play Publishing, 2019

Howe, Andrew, *Encyclopedia of Socceroos Centenary Edition*, Fair Play Publishing, 2022

Slater, Robbie & Hall, Matthew, *The Hard Way*, Harper Sports, 1999

Wright, Ian, *My Life in Football*, Constable, 2016

Celtic View

Ozfootball.net

Melbournesoccer.blogspot.com

Transfermarkt.com

Espn.com.au

Theinnersanctum.com.au

Soccer Action

Soccer World

Sydney Morning Herald

TheWorldGame.sbs.com.au

The Age

Canberra Times

Australian Soccer Weekly

Melbourneknights.com.au

Ftbl.com.au

Optus Sport

BBC

Just Women's Sports, with Kelley O'Hara

Shim, Spider and so much Moore, with Simon Hill, Zeljko Kalac and Craig Moore

The Pioneers, Football Nation Radio, with George Cotsanis and George Donikian

FCA Football Coaching Life, with Gary Cole

footballaustralia.com.au.

About the Author

Jason Goldsmith lives in the inner north of Melbourne; a father of two, he is heavily involved in community sport and a big fan of Australian footballers and the national teams. He loves nothing more than watching the progress of the Socceroos and Matildas at World and Asian Cups.

Green and Golden Boots is his third book following *Surfing for England* (2019) and *Be My Guest* (2021) which was co-written with Lucas Gillard. All three books and many more really good football books are available via Fair Play Publishing.

Jason with Aurelio Vidmar at the 2010 World Cup in South Africa.

More really good football books from Fair Play Publishing

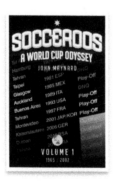

Ingram Content Group UK Ltd.
Milton Keynes UK
UKHW020729030723
424465UK00004B/22